ACTS

AND

RESOLUTIONS

OF THE

NATIONAL COUNCIL

OF THE

MUSKOGEE NATION

OF

1893 AND 1899, INCLUSIVE.

Scholarly Resources Inc.
1508 Pennsylvania Avenue · Wilmington, Delaware 19806

SCHOLARLY RESOURCES, INC.
Wilmington, Delaware • London

Reprint edition published in 1975

Library of Congress Catalog Card Number: 75-3697
ISBN: 0-8420-1888-3

Manufactured in the United States of America

ACTS

AND

RESOLUTIONS

OF THE

NATIONAL COUNCIL

OF THE

MUSKOGEE NATION

OF

1893 AND 1899, INCLUSIVE.

MUSKOGEE, IND. TER.:
PHOENIX PRINTING COMPANY,
1900.

PREFACE.

The Acts and Resolutions in this volume are merely a reprint as they appeared in pamphlet form in 1893 and '96, with the Acts and Resolutions of 1897, '98 and '99 added thereto. The Acts are printed in the order of their passage. There was no attempt made at classification. Quite a number of the Acts and Resolutions are, gramatically, incomplete and incorrect, but no changes were made in that respect. The sole object in printing the laws has been to embody in convenient form in one volume all the Acts and Resolutions of the Council from 1893 to 1899 inclusive. The work has been done by direction of P. Porter, Principal Chief of the Creek Nation.

A. P. McKELLOP.

ACTS AND RESOLUTIONS
MUSKOGEE NATION.

ACTS AND RESOLUTIONS OF 1893—AUTHORIZING THE PRINTING OF.

SECTION 1. The Principal Chief is hereby authorized and directed to appoint some competent person to compile all the laws passed by the present session of Council and have the same translated correctly into Creek and have them printed in one volume in pamphlet form.

SEC. 2. The work of compiling, translating and printing shall be done as soon after the adjournment of the present session of Council as possible. There shall be a thousand copies printed and one sent to each officer and member of Council and the balance shall be equally distributed to the several towns.

SEC. 3. For the purpose of carrying this act into effect there is hereby appropriated the sum of five hundred dollars ($500), or so much thereof as shall be necessary; and the Principal Chief shall report to Council the manner of the disbursement of the said amount.

SEC. 4. The needed corrections pointed out by the special committee appointed to examine the new compilation of the laws shall be included in the compilation and translation herein provided for.

Approved November 6, 1893.

L. C. PERRYMAN, Principal Chief.

EAST AND WEST RAILROAD.

SEC. 5. It is the opinion of the National Council of the Muskogee Nation, that the construction, by a company duly authorized by Congress, of a branch railroad from a point on the eastern boundary of the Muskogee Nation, running westward to connect with the Missouri, Kansas & Texas railroad at some point between Muskogee and Eufaula, so as to form a continuous road, in conjunction with the main line, to our southern boundary, is in accordance with the stipulations of the Treaty of June 14, 1866, between the Muskogee Nation and the United States, which concedes the "right of way to any company which shall be duly authorized by Congress, and shall, with the express consent of the Secretary of the Interior, undertake to construct a railroad from * * * * any point on their eastern to their southern or western boundary" as the same completes and exhausts all railroad grants and franchises conceded by existing Treaties between the United States and the Muskogee Nation; *provided, however*, that nothing herein shall be so construed as to infer any expression of opinion in regard to the question as to what company may be duly authorized by Congress.

Approved November 2, 1881.

CORRECTIONS—COMPILED LAWS, 1893.

SEC. 6. Section 324 should read: "The Captain shall then post and advertise all estray stock reported to him for the period of six months, *giving due notice of time and place of sale*, and sell the same at public sale to the highest bidder for National warrants, scrip or cash."

SEC. 7. To Section 329 should be added: "and shall pay one-third of the amount for which the same shall have been sold to the purchaser from whom he proves the stock."

To Section 115 should be added: "And the District Judge shall file a bond of two thousand dollars ($2,000.00.)"

SEC. 8. In chapter 20, edition 1893, for adopted citizens, substitute the name of Thos. Hawkins for Lizzie Hawkins; Josephine Freeman for Josephine Bruner; and M. A. Rickets for M. O. Rickets.

GAME—PROHIBITING HUNTING WITH UNITED STATES CITIZENS.

SEC. 9. Should any citizen of this Nation be found hunting game in this Nation in company with any United

States citizen, he shall be liable to a fine of not less than one hundred dollars ($100.00).

SEC. 10. The prosecuting attorneys of the several districts shall prosecute all citizens violating this law.

Became a law by limitation, 1891.

FENCE—LAWFUL FARM.

SEC. 11. A lawful rail fence shall be seven rails high, well staked and double-ridered.

SEC. 12. A straight fence, built of six rails or poles, whether fastened to posts with wire or nails, with two strands of wire stretched above the rails, shall be deemed a lawful fence.

SEC. 13. A lawful wire fence shall be of eight wires attached to posts eight feet apart and one stay between each two posts. The bottom wire shall be four inches above the ground, the second three inches above the first, the third four inches above the second, the fourth six inches above the third, the fifth seven inches above the fourth, the sixth eight inches above the fifth, the seventh twelve inches above the sixth, and the eighth fourteen inches above the seventh. The height shall be four feet and ten inches, with strong corner posts well braced.

SEC. 14. When any citizen shall have a lawful fence as defined in this act, and the stock or property of another citizen shall damage or injure his crops, he shall be entitled to damages for such injury, which shall be assessed by two disinterested persons, said persons to be appointed by the Judge of the District wherein said damage is done.

SEC. 15. No citizen not having a lawful fence shall be entitled to damages done to his crops by the stock of another.

Approved October 11, 1893.

LAND—LEASING OF PROHIBITED.

Sec. 16. It shall be unlawful for any citizen of this Nation to lease for a term of years any portion of the unoccupied domain to any non-citizen to be occupied or improved by the non-citizen at his own expense in consideration of his occupancy and use of said land for said term of years.

Sec. 17. If any person shall violate this law he shall, upon conviction before the District Court, forfeit all such improvement to the Nation and be laible to a fine of one hundred dollars ($100.00.)

Approved November 6, 1893.

TIMBER LAW—AMENDMENT TO.

Sec. 18. Section 400 of the timber law found on page 133 of the law book, edition 1893, shall not be so construed as to invest any person with the personal right or title to timber or land within the half-mile limit therein mentioned, but the same shall be public domain for all purposes other than for making railroad ties as provided for in the said act.

Approved October 24, 1893.

WALNUT TIMBER LAW—AMENDMENT TO.

Sec. 19. The act of the National Council, approved October, 1889, found on page 60 of law book, edition 1890, authorizing Snow Sells to take charge of and dispose of all down walnut timber, is hereby repealed.

Sec. 20. Section 155 of the law found on page 60 of the law book, edition 1893, prohibiting the selling of walnut timber and fixing a penalty for violation of the same, is hereby so amended that any person failing to pay the fine therein provided for shall receive fifty lashes on the bare back for each and every offense, and if any officer shall be found guilty of a violation of this act he shall, upon conviction before the court, be removed from office in addition to the payment of said fine.

Approved October 24, 1893.

PRIMARY SCHOOLS—GRADES OF.

After the 30th of May, 1894, the following law shall be in force:

SEC. 21. There shall be three grades of Primary Schools, namely: First, Second and Third.

SEC. 22. There shall be fifteen of the first grade, to average twenty in attendance; twenty-five of the second grade, to average fifteen; and twenty-five of the third grade, to average ten.

SEC. 23. Teachers of the first grade shall receive $35.00 per month; of the second grade $30.00 per month; of the third grade $25.00 per month.

SEC. 24. The teachers shall be given graded certificates, and appointed to schools accordingly.

SEC. 25. The Board of Education is hereby authorized to make such rules and regulations as will best facilitate the grading and appointing of schools and teachers.

Approved October 19, 1893.

SCHOOLS—SUPERINTENDENTS OF BOARDING, AND BOARD OF EDUCATION.

SEC. 26. The superintendents of the intermediate and high schools shall be nominated by the Chief and confirmed by Council. They must be persons of good moral character and competency, and shall be liable to impeachment.

SEC. 27. The superintendent of any intermediate or high school shall be responsible for any indebtedness he may incur for his school, which may exceed the regular appropriation for said school.

SEC. 28. He shall take his position upon the 5th of

December next following his election and shall hold his office for the term of two years.

SEC. 29. He shall have a right, with the approval of the trustees, to select the teachers and employes for his school, the teachers to hold certificates from the board, and may discharge any teacher or employe for incompetency or immoral conduct, and replace same with the approval of the trustees.

SEC. 30. The salary of superintendent of schools accommodating 100 pupils shall be $700.00; of schools accommodating 50 pupils, $500.00; of the Creek Orphan Asylum, $700.00; of the Colored Orphan Asylum, $500.00 per annum, to be paid quarterly as to other standing officers.

SEC. 31. The books for the intermediate and high schools shall be paid for out of the regular appropriation for their respective schools.

SEC. 32. The members of the board shall be liable to impeachment.

SEC. 33. The Chief shall have power to suspend any member of the board or any superintendent upon sufficient charges being made, and may appoint a substitute to hold the office until the following Council.

SEC. 34. The board shall not accept the report of superintendent when vouchers do not accompany, and shall issue no order for warrant until proper report is made, and if the board issue such order without proper vouchers the members of the board shall be responsible to that amount.

SEC. 35. This law shall not be so construed as to deprive any superintendent now in office of his position, but shall confirm his appointment for the ensuing year.

SEC. 36. From and after the passage of this act it shall be in full force and virtue.

Approved November 1, 1893.

ORPHANS—HOW ADMITTED TO ASYLUMS.

SEC. 37. Any orphan may be admitted into an asylum at any age over eight and under eighteen years, and shall be compelled to remain there under the authority of the superintendent until they shall have attained the age of twenty-one years, unless continued sickness or improper conduct compels them to leave.

Provided, however, That any orphan over twelve years old who may have business at home requiring their attention shall be allowed to return home during the vacation, and *provided*, that if any orphan who is in an asylum has a guardian who wishes to enter said orphan in a higher school, such guardian shall have the right to do so.

SEC. 38. The trustees of the asylums shall be required to keep the asylum full according to law having in view the appropriation for same.

Approved November 6, 1893.

NUYAKA MISSION—TO DISSOLVE CONTRACT WITH PRESBYTERIAN BOARD.

SEC. 39. Be it resolved by the National Council of the Muskogee Nation, That the Board of Education be and is hereby instructed and directed to give notice of a dissolution of the contract of 1893 with the Presbyterian Board of Home Missions regarding Nuyaka Mission, which dissolution shall take place upon the end of the present school term of the said school.

Approved November 1, 1893.

INSPECTOR, LIVE STOCK—AMENDING ACT RELATING TO.

SEC. 40. The term of office of the live stock inspector shall be two years.

SEC. 41. He shall be elected by Council.

SEC. 42. He shall file a bond with the National Treasurer in the sum of twenty thousand dollars ($20,000.00). He shall report to the National Council annually all moneys accruing under his office.

Approved October 19, 1893.

LICENSE LAW—AMENDMENT TO.

Sec. 43. The license tax law is hereby so amended as to include the following taxes:

Sewing Machine Co., per year	$25.00
Auctioneers in house or tent, per day	3.00
Auctioneers on street, per day	2.00
Dime shows, per week	1.00

Approved October 27, 1893.

PECANS—GATHERING BY NON-CITIZENS PROHIBITED.

Sec. 44. The Principal Chief of the Muskogee Nation is hereby authorized and directed to request the United States Indian Agent to prohibit all non-citizens from gathering and selling pecans from off the public domain.

Approved October 25, 1893.

IMDIGENTS—LAW RELATING TO AMENDED.

Sec. 45. The resolution defining who are indigents and entitled to money from the Nation as such, shall be so amended as to read, "No person drawing money as pension from the United States Government shall be entitled to any money from this Nation under the head of indigent."

Approved October 19, 1893.

ASSISTANT LIGHT HORSEMEN—EMPLOYMENT OF BY JUDGE PROHIBITED.

Sec. 46. From and after the passage of this act no District Judge shall have the right to employ or use any assistant Light Horsemen; and if any Judge shall violate this law he shall be immediately suspended from office by the Principal Chief; and if any person shall serve as assistant Light Horseman under appointment from any Judge he shall not be paid by the Nation.

Approved November 6, 1893.

GRANTS TO RAILROADS—URGING REPEAL OF ACTS RELATING TO.

SEC. 47. In the event of the election of a delegation to represent the interests of this Nation at Washington, they are hereby authorized and directed to earnestly urge the proper authorities of the United States to repeal so much of the acts of Congress approved respectively July 25, 26 and 27, 1866, authorizing the construction of certain railroads through the Indian Territory, and as grants to such railroad companies, giving each alternate section of land of our present domain for twenty miles on each side of such railroads.

Approved November 6, 1893.

PRINCIPAL CHIEF—ELECTION OF BY MAJORITY.

SEC. 48. From and after the 5th of December, 1891, no person shall be entitled to any election to the office of Principal Chief, who, at an election lawfully held, shall not have received a majority of all the votes cast as contemplated by a strict construction of the letter of the Constitution bearing upon the subject of the election of the Principal Chief.

Became a law by limitation, 1891.

CLERKS OF COURTS—PROHIBITING THEIR PRACTICE OF LAW.

SEC. 49. No Judge of any of the Courts of this Nation shall allow the clerk of his Court to practice law before his Court; and for a violation of this act he shall be subject to removal from office.

Approved October 26, 1893.

ATTORNEY GENERAL—ELECTION AND DUTIES OF.

SEC. 50. A competent attorney at law, well versed in the laws of the Creek Nation and conversant with both the

English and Creek languages, shall be elected by the National Council at its present session, whose duty shall be to institute suit or suits before the Supreme Court against any person or officer, owing the Nation any sum of money for any purpose or on any account whatever, and to prosecute such cases vigorously and have the same commenced before the next June term of the Supreme Court. The said attorney shall file a bond of ten thousand dollars ($10,000.00) before the Principal Chief, conditioned upon the faithful discharge of his duties as such attorney. The said attorney shall have the authority to direct the Judges of the several Districts to execute his orders and the judgment of the Supreme Court and if any judgment be rendered against any person or officer in default with the Nation and a collection of the judgment is attempted, the exemption law as appears in Chapter XIII, pages 90 and 91, edition, 1893, shall not be construed so as to operate against the collection of said judgment. The said attorney shall be allowed his actual traveling expenses and boarding expenses and also 25 per cent. of all moneys secured by him for the Nation, and turned into the National Treasury. The said attorney shall serve for two years from the 5th of December, 1893. He shall make annual report to the National Council.

Approved November 3, 1893.

COMMISSIONERS—TO TAKE CENSUS OF NON-CITIZENS AND EFFECT THEIR REMOVAL.

SEC. 51. There is hereby created a commission to be composed of three competent persons to be elected by the National Council and to continue in office from their election to the annual session of Council of 1894. They shall visit every non-citizen residing in this Nation and register the names of each member of each family, their race or color, and an inventory of all live stock, held or claimed by them.

They shall ascertain as near as may be, without an actual survey thereof, the number of acres of all lands enclosed for farms, pastures, orchards, gardens, town or other lots, together with all other improvements such as houses, barns or sheds occupied, held or owned by them; the particular occupation of each and the authority under which each claim to own, occupy or enjoy the properties herein mentioned. They shall also ascertain the origin, nature and character of any right, title or privileges claimed in or to such live stock, farm, pasture or other improvement and render a full report in detail to the next regular session of the National Council.

SEC. 52. In order to more effectually carry into operation the provisions of this act, the United States Indian Agent of the Union Agency is hereby requested to detail one of his policemen to accompany each commissioner, if he shall need one, to aid in serving any summons he may find necessary to issue for the appearance of persons needed in making the investigations herein provided for; each commissioner shall also, in cases of actual necessity have the right to the services of the Light Horse Company of the District wherein he may be at work, and the District Judges are hereby instructed to honor any requisition made by him for such service in the legal discharge of such duties herein imposed upon him.

SEC. 53. If the Commissioners shall find any non-citizen residing in this country contrary to the Treaties, the United States statutes or the laws of this country, they shall report the same to the Indian Agent and request his removal from the country, and if for any cause the Agent shall fail either to act, or cause his removal within a reasonable time, the Commissioner shall then report the matter to the Interior Department and ask his removal.

SEC. 54. That portion of the law requiring district solicitors to report intruders to the Indian Agent is hereby repealed, *provided*, that nothing herein contained shall be construed so as to interfere with the additional one hundred dollars ($100.00) per annum allowed solicitors by said law.

SEC. 55. The pay of each Commissioner is hereby fixed at three dollars ($3.00) per day, and that of the policeman at one dollar ($1.00) per day, provided that no greater amount in the aggregate than one thousand dollars ($1,000.00) shall be paid to any Commissioner and his assistant during his term of office.

Approved November 3, 1893.

UNITED STATES COMMISSIONERS—RESOLUTIONS TO BE PRESENTED TO.

SEC. 56. It is the sense of this body that any change in the present status of the Indian Territory that would include the Muskogee Nation within the limits of an organized State of the American Union, would be contrary to the best interests of the citizens of the Nation, and any proposition of Congress to effect such a change or to include this Nation in any State or Territory wherein the present Territory of Oklahoma shall be a component part is greatly to be deprecated and resisted by all proper means.

SEC. 57. The Principal Chief is hereby instructed to furnish copies of these resolutions to any commission or committee that may be sent out to visit this Territory under act of the last regular session of Congress, to the Secretary of the Interior and to the United States Indian Agent at Muskogee.

Approved November 1, 1893.

PER CAPITA PAYMENT OF $600,000.00.

SEC. 58. $600,000.00 of the money, ($2,000,000.00), derived from the sale of the Oklahoma lands and now standing to the credit of the Muskogee Nation with the United States Government, shall be withdrawn and be distributed per capita to the citizens of the Muskogee Nation.

SEC. 59. The National Council now in session shall immediately proceed to enact legislation to make this act effective.

Approved October 24, 1893.

REQUISITION FOR $600,000.00.

SEC. 60. The Principal Chief is hereby authorized and directed, for and on behalf of the Muskogee Nation, to make requisition upon the proper authorities of the United States in such forms as may be necessary or required by the said authorities for the payment to the National Treasurer of the Muskogee Nation, of the sum of $600,000.00, out of the amount of money in the Treasury of the United States to the credit of the Muskogee Nation on account of the sale to the United States, under act of cession and agreement entered into January 19, 1889, of the lands ceded to the United States under treaty, 1866. Such requisition when made shall be taken and accepted and is hereby declared to be the requisition of the proper authorities of the Muskogee Nation.

Appproved November 4, 1893.

COLBY, L. W.—EMPLOYMENT OF AS ATTORNEY.

SEC. 61. Hon. Leonard W. Colby, an attorney of long standing, of Washington, D. C., is hereby employed as attorney for the Muskogee Nation to defend the interests of the Muskogee Nation in all suits pending or that may hereafter be brought in the Court of Claims or the Supreme Court of the United States for Indian depredations, for the term of three years, at an annual salary of four thousand dollars ($4,000.00.)

SEC. 62. The Principal Chief of the Muskogee Nation is hereby authorized and directed to enter into a written contract with said attorney on behalf of said Nation for such employment.

SEC. 63. There is hereby appropriated an amount for the payment of said salary and the Principal Chief is authorized to issue warrants therefor and the National Treasurer to pay the same from the funds of the National Treasury as provided by law.

Approved November 6, 1893.

BOUNDARY LINE BETWEEN EUFAULA AND MUSKOGEE DISTRICTS.

SEC. 64. The Principal Chief is hereby authorized and directed to appoint two disinterested persons, not residents of either Eufaula or Muskogee Districts to go to the boundary line between the two Districts and beginning at Hopoethle Yoholar's cow pen run the line to Soda Springs, defining same by posts or stakes, and report to present Council.

Approved October 14, 1893.

BOUNDARY LINE BETWEEN EUFAULA AND MUSKOGEE DISTRICTS—REPORT ON ADOPTED.

SEC. 65. The District boundary line between the Eufaula and Muskogee Districts, as traced and established by Cæsar Rogers and Marsey Harjo, so as to run 220 feet North of W. E. Gentry & Co's. store and 143 feet North of Fisher Mercantile Co's. store, is hereby accepted and declared to be the correct boundary between the said Districts; the said Rogers and Harjo being appointed surveyors under the above act.

Approved October 24, 1893.

ATTACHMENT—OF PROPERTY IN LITIGATION.

SEC. 66. From and after the passage of this act when a case has been instituted in any District Court or in the Supreme Court and the plaintiff has reason to believe that the property in dispute is about to be disposed of by sale or otherwise, or to be removed from the limits of this Nation for the purpose of defeating any judgment which may be rendered by the Court, he may apply to the Court for a writ of injunction restraining the defendant from disposing of such property.

SEC. 67. Before such injunction or attachment can issue, the plaintiff shall state under oath, with not less than two witnesses, that such property is about to be disposed of or removed, and also file a bond with not less than two responsible sureties in a sum twice the amount of property to be attached, for the payment of such damage or damages as may be sustained by the defendant in case the plaintiff fails to gain his suit.

SEC. 68. If any defendant in any cause shall dispose of any property by sale, removal from the country or otherwise after the same has been attached or enjoined by order of the Court, he shall be deemed guilty of larceny and shall be punished accordingly.

Approved November 6, 1893.

NEW CONSTITUTION—TO BE DRAFTED AND VOTED ON.

SEC. 69. All the male citizens of voting age of the several towns shall meet in their respective towns at the usual place of meeting on the 15th day of December, 1893, and and shall then and there proceed to elect two delegates to represent their towns and the delegates thus elected shall meet at Okmulgee, M. N., on the first Tuesday in January, 1894, and then and there organize by electing a chairman from one of their number and a clerk and interpreter from outside.

SEC. 70. The said delegation, when thus organized, shall proceed to prepare and draft a new Constitution for the Muskogee Nation, which when completed shall be submitted to the Principal Chief.

SEC. 71. When the Principal Chief shall receive the

proposed new Constitution he shall have the same carefully translated and printed in both English and Creek, and shall send a copy of each to every Town Chief, and shall also order the Town Chiefs to call a meeting of all voters in their respective towns and to submit to them the new Constitution for adoption or rejection by popular vote. The Town Chiefs shall call the voters of their towns to meet on the second Tuesday in June, 1894, to vote on said Constitution. The Principal Chief shall furnish the necessary blanks and the votes shall be recorded in duplicate, one copy to be held by the Town Chief and the other to be forwarded to the President of the House of Kings, and the President of the House of Kings shall submit all such returns to the National Council at its regular session in October, 1894.

SEC. 72. If the Constitution, as herein above provided for shall be ratified by a majority vote of the people, then the Principal Chief shall promulgate the same by proclamation and thereupon it shall become and be the Constitution of the Muskogee Nation, *provided, however*, that nothing therein contained shall be taken, construed or held to in any way interfere with the present Constitution and laws, or any officer now in office until after the expiration of the present Constitutional term of Council, *except, however*, that the next general election for the election of Principal Chief and Second Chief, and members of the Council shall be held in accordance with the new Constitution.

SEC. 73. The said delegates shall each receive two dollars ($2.00) per day while in attendance at the meeting and mileage at the rate of ten cents (10c.) per mile in going to and returning from the Capitol. The clerk and interpreter shall receive the same per diem and mileage as the delegates.

SEC. 74. The convention of delegates herein provided for, shall not sit longer than twenty days, exclusive of Sundays.

SEC. 75. For the purpose of carrying this act into effect there is hereby appropriated the sum of five thousand dollars ($5,000.00), or so much thereof as may be necessary.

Approved November 1, 1893.

NON-CITIZENS, INTERMARRIED—COURTS TO HAVE JURISDICTION OF THEIR PROPERTY.

SEC. 76. The courts of this Nation shall have and exercise jurisdiction over all controversies arising out of or pertaining to property rights acquired in this Nation, and situated in the same, by non-citizens who have intermarried with citizens of this Nation and by reason of such marriage secured rights and privileges in this Nation under which such property was acquired and accumulated by them. The jurisdiction of our courts shall extend to controversies over property and property rights acquired by intermarried non-citizens of our Nation who, by virtue of this intermarriage with citizens, acquired such property rights and privileges, and that irrespective of whether such controversies are between non-citizens and citizens of the Muskogee Nation or between any person whomsoever, who claim in this Nation property rights under and through such intermarried non-citizens which are by them acquired in the manner aforesaid; and all persons hereafter intermarrying with citizens of this Nation shall thereby be deemed to consent that the courts of this Nation exercise jurisdiction over all property rights and privileges that they acquire in this Nation by virtue of their said marriage.

SEC. 77. All property brought into this Nation by non-citizens in consequence of intermarriage of such non-citizens with citizens of this Nation shall likewise be under the jurisdiction of the courts of this Nation.

Approved April 6, 1894.

SUPERINTENDENTS OF BOARDING SCHOOLS—TERM OF OFFICE FIXED.

Sec. 78. The law providing for election of Superintendents of Boarding Schools, found in the pamphlet edition, April, 1894, be so amended as to make the next ensuing term of their office one year instead of two.

Sec. 79. After the next general election the said law shall resume its full force and virtue.

DEAD BODIES—PENALTY FOR DISINTERMENT OF.

Sec. 80. Every person who shall remove the dead body of any human being from the grave or other place of interment for the purpose of stealing the same or for the purpose of dissection or from mere wantonness, shall be deemed guilty of a misdemeanor.

Sec. 81. Every person who shall purchase or receive the dead body of any human being knowing the same to have been disinterred contrary to law, shall be guilty of a misdemeanor.

Sec. 82. Every person who shall open a grave or other place of interment with the intent to remove the dead body of any human being, for the purpose of stealing the coffin or any part thereof, or the vestments or other articles or money interred with any dead body shall be deemed guilty of a misdemeanor.

Sec. 83. Persons convicted of any offense specified in the preceding sections shall be fined one hundred dollars, and in addition thereto suffer the penalty of fifty lashes on the bare back. Fifty dollars of said fine to be paid to the heirs of the deceased and fifty dollars to be transmitted to the National Treasurer. It shall be the duty of the Prosecuting Attorneys of the several Districts to prosecute all persons violating this act.

Approved October 12, 1894.

CITIZENS, ADOPTED—TO RECEIVE NO PAY FOR PROPERTY CONFISCATED PRIOR TO ADOPTION.

SEC. 84. Any person making application for indemnity occurring by confiscation of property or improvements that has occurred before his or her admission to citizenship to this Nation is hereby debarred from receiving any compensation out of the National Treasury on account of said loss.

This act shall be in force from and after its approval.

Approved October 12, 1894.

MILEAGE—OF MEMBERS AND CLERKS OF COUNCIL AND CLERKS OF COURTS.

SEC. 85. The law found on page 36, Section 77, of the edition of 1893, be and is hereby so amended as to make the mileage of the members of the National Council and the regular clerks and interpreters ten (10) cents per mile each way instead of twenty (20) cents.

SEC. 86. Section 97, found on page 43, edition of 1893, be so amended as to allow the Clerk and Caller ten (10) cents per mile each way going to and returning from the sessions of the Supreme Court.

SEC. 87. Section 115, on page 49, edition of 1893, be so amended as to make the mileage of jurors and witnesses in criminal cases ten (10) cents per mile going to and returning from court.

SEC. 88. This act shall be in full force from and after the first of November, 1894, and the Principal Chief is hereby authorized and instructed to furnish the several District Judges with a copy of this act.

Approved October 16, 1894.

DISTRICT COURTS—FIXING SESSIONS OF.

SEC. 89. For the trial of such criminal cases as may arise, each District Court shall have three sessions annually, to commence as follows:

EUFAULA DISTRICT.

First session..Second Monday in February.
Second session ....First Monday in June.
Third session ....Second Monday in November.

WEWOKA DISTRICT.

First session..Second Monday in April.
Second session ....Third Monday in July.
Third session ....First Monday in December.

MUSKOGEE DISTRICT.

First session..First Monday in January.
Second session....................................Third Monday in May.
Third session.......................................Second Monday in September.

OKMULGEE DISTRICT.

First session..Third Monday in March.
Second session....................................First Monday in July.
Third session.......................................Fourth Monday in November.

DEEP FORK DISTRICT.

First session..Third Monday in January.
Second session....................................First Monday in May.
Third session ....Second Monday in August.

COWETA DISTRICT.

First session..First Monday in February.
Second session .... First Monday in June.
Third session.......................................First Monday in November.

SEC. 90. Should any District Judge, by sickness or other hindrance, be prevented from holding court at any time specified by this law, he shall call a session at as near that time as he may deem best; but no District Court shall sit at one session for a longer time than fifteen days; *provided*, that murder cases may be tried at any time.

Approved October 19, 1894.

MARRIAGE AND DIVORCE LAW—DATE OF APPROVAL CORRECTED.

SEC. 91. The date of approval of the Marriage and Divorce law of the Muskogee Nation, found on pages 108 and 109 of the English compilation and codification of the Laws of the Muskogee Nation, of 1893, is hereby declared error of print and is hereby corrected and fixed at October 22, 1881, instead of 1891.

Approved October 19, 1894.

SUBPŒNAS—PENALTY FOR FAILURE TO OBEY.

SEC. 92. If any witness shall fail to appear before the District Court or the Supreme Court, either in criminal or civil cases, on the day on which he was subpœnaed to appear, he shall be fined in the sum of twenty-five ($25.00) dollars.

SEC. 93. The Judges of the District Courts and the Chief Justice of the Supreme Court shall assess the fines against the delinquent witnesses before their respective courts, and they shall order the Light Horsemen to collect the fines, which shall be paid within ten days after the assessment is made, and no property shall be exempt from seizure and forced sale to satisfy said fine.

SEC. 94. The District Judges and the Chief Justice of the Supreme Court shall each file a bond in the penal sum of five hundred ($500.00) dollars with the Principal Chief with approved security, conditioned that they will faithfully collect all fines due and make proper disposition of same.

SEC. 95. That all fines collected under this act by the District Judges shall be expended under their direction for the repairs and improvement of the court houses and for buying necessary furniture and fixtures for same and for building fences around the court house and other like improvements; and all fines collected by the Chief Justice of the Supreme Court shall be turned over to the National Treasurer.

SEC. 96. The Nation shall not pay the mileage and per diem of more than three witnesses in criminal cases on part of the Government and the same on part of the defendants.

SEC. 97. The District Judges and the Chief Justice of the Supreme Court shall each report annually to the National Council the amount of fines collected and the disposition made of same.

SEC. 98. Nothing herein contained shall be construed as to assess a fine against any person who fails to obey a legal subpœna by reason of sickness of himself or family.

Approved October 22, 1894.

ORPHAN ASYLUM, CREEK—SETTING ASIDE LAND FOR.

SEC. 99. There shall be and is hereby set apart a tract of land, not to exceed 640 acres, for the Creek Orphan Asylum, to be used as farm, garden, orchard and pasture. Said land to be measured and set apart by the Board of Education before the first day of January, 1895.

Approved October 23, 1894.

ENCLOSURES NEAR CAPITOL BUILDING—TO BE REMOVED.

SEC. 100. The Light Horse Company of Okmulgee District be, and they are hereby, directed to at once enforce the law prohibiting persons from enclosing fields or pastures within one-half mile of the Capitol building.

SEC. 101. The Light Horsemen of said District are hereby further directed and authorized to take down and remove all fences built within one-half mile since the passage and approval of said act prohibiting such enclosure.

Approved October 6, 1894.

INSPECTORS, DISTRICT—LAW CREATING.

SEC. 102. There be and is hereby created the office of District Inspector, one for each of the six Districts, who shall be nominated by the Principal Chief and confirmed by the National Council, who shall hold his office for the term of two years, who shall be charged with the duty of collecting permit taxes and issuing all permits for non-citizen labor.

SEC. 103. From and after the passage of this act any citizen of this Nation who shall desire to employ any non-citizen of this Nation, shall, before doing so, be required to comply with the following regulations in all cases where the non-citizen is of the age of eighteen years and over: He shall first obtain a permit from the District Inspector, as specified in this act; and any citizen employing a non-citizen without first obtaining a permit shall be guilty of a misdemeanor, and the absence in the files of the Inspector's office of a written contract or agreement between such citizen and any non-citizen found in his employ shall, for the purposes of this act, be sufficient evidence of his violation of this law and his liability to the penalty of a fine of twelve ($12.00) dollars.

SEC. 104. It shall be the duty of the District Inspector to report all violations of this law to the Judge of the District, whose duty it shall be to order his Light Horsemen to proceed at once and collect the fine imposed and turn the same into the National Treasury. He shall have and exercise all the duties and authority conferred upon the Commissioners created by the act of 1893 respecting the removal of non-citizens or intruders from the Nation. The said Inspectors shall have the right to appoint each a competent clerk, who shall be a citizen of the Muskogee Nation and whose duty shall be to keep a correct record and file of all business of the office. The said Inspectors and their clerks shall receive each 25 per cent. of all moneys collected by them as compensation for their services.

SEC. 105. All citizens employing the services of any non-citizen of the age of 18 years and over shall be required to pay a permit, and no permit shall be issued for a longer period than twelve (12) months. All permits shall be renewed within ten (10) days after their expiration.

Sec. 106. The tax for common labor shall be one ($1.00) dollar per month; for mechanics one dollar and twenty-five cents; non-citizen clerks and accountants in the employ of licensed traders shall be required to pay a monthly tax of fifty (50) cents.

Sec. 107. Any non-citizen who holds a permit under the provisions of this act shall be permitted to hold and graze upon the public domain ten (10) head of work stock and three head of milch cows and calves free of taxation, and all hogs kept and owned by such employed non-citizen shall be confined in enclosures not to exceed two (2) acres in extent; and any greater number of work or other stock found ranging on the public domain and belonging to an employed non-citizen shall subject the citizen employing him to all the pains and penalties provided in Section 335 of the quarantine laws of the Nation.

Sec. 108. No non-citizen shall be permitted to own houses or fences of any kind within the Nation, or any interest therein; and any purchase, grant, lease or other conveyance of lands of the Muskogee Nation, or title or claim thereto given by any citizen or person claiming to be a citizen, contrary to Section 2116 of the United States Intercourse Laws, is hereby declared to be null, void and of no effect.

Sec. 109. The provisions of this act shall not confer the right on a permitted non-citizen to cut and sell wood, hay, rails or boards or mine and sell coal or dispose of any of the natural products of this Nation for his personal benefit, and any violation of this law shall subject such permitted non-citizen to a forfeiture of all rights and privileges accruing under the provisions of this act, and to a forfeiture to the Nation of all such coal, timber, wood or other products.

SEC. 110. Each District Inspector shall, before entering upon the duties of his office, file with the National Treasurer a bond of one thousand ($1,000.00) dollars, with approved security, conditioned upon the faithful performance of his duties as herein specified, as well as an honest and prompt payment to the National Treasurer at the end of each quarter of all funds—less fees—collected from permits. He shall make a full and correct report of the business of his office quarterly to the Treasurer. If he shall fail to render his quarterly report within fifteen days after the close of any quarter, he shall be reported by the Treasurer to the Principal Chief for removal, who shall at once remove him and fill the vancancy by a temporary appointment.

The District Inspector shall also make an annual report of the business of his office to the National Council.

SEC. 111. The District Inspectors are hereby required to immediately report to each other the names of all non-citizens whose permits have been by them revoked or refused, and no Inspector shall for such non-citizen issue a permit, under penalty of a forfeiture of his bond.

The District Inspector shall refuse to issue any permit to a non-citizen when legal objections have been filed by any citizen, and shall revoke any permit when the party for whom the same has been issued is shown to be an unfit person to remain in our Nation and shall declare and proceed against him as an intruder.

It shall also be the duty of the District Inspector to require a written agreement between employer and employe before issuing a permit to any non-citizen, said contract to become a matter of record in the Inspector's office.

SEC. 112. Nothing in this act shall be so construed as to prevent the employment of teachers by the Board of Education. No property except improvements shall be exempt from payment of the fine hereby imposed for violations of the provisions of this law, and all laws and parts of laws in conflict herewith are hereby repealed.

Approved October 30, 1894.

COLBY, L. W.—REPEAL OF ACT OF EMPLOYMENT.

SEC. 113. The act of the Council of November 6, 1893, by which Hon. L. W. Colby, of Washington, D. C., was employed in certain suits pending and that may hereafter be brought in the Court of Claims or Supreme Court of the United States for Indian depredation claims, be and the same is hereby repealed, and no draft or drafts or warrant or warrants of the Nation shall be issued under provisions of said act on any account whatsoever; and the Principal Chief is hereby directed to serve due notice to said L. W. Colby of his dismissal.

Approved October 30, 1894.

COAL LAW—ACT AMENDATORY TO.

An act amendatory to an act approved December 3, 1887, providing for the mining of coal in the Muskogee Nation for said purpose.

SEC. 114. All minerals existing in their natural state within the limits of the Muskogee Nation are the property of said Nation and subject to its disposition and control.

SEC. 115. The act of December 3, 1887, is hereby made to include such as salt, oil, natural gas, medicinal waters, and all other minerals except gold and silver, and such companies as may organize for the purpose of engaging in the mining of any of said minerals shall first incorporate under and in the manner provided for by the law to which this act is amendatory in so far as it may be applicable to the mining of the different variety of minerals, granting to such companies only those rights and privileges necessary to the successful operating, refining and marketing of said minerals.

SEC. 116. The tax or royalty which shall accrue to the Nation from said mining companies, payable according to the provisions of act of December 3, 1888, shall hereafter be as follows: On all coal minerals, five cents per ton; on rock or stone, three cents per ton; on oil, four cents for each barrel of fifty gallons; on natural gas, twenty-five dollars per annum for each well from which gas is sold; and on all other minerals, five per cent. of the value of such minerals at the place of production.

SEC. 117. All companies organizing and operating under this act and the law to which it is amendatory shall be required first to file a bond with the Principal Chief in the penal sum of not less than ten thousand dollars, conditioned upon the requirements of the law to which this act is amendatory.

SEC. 118. All acts or parts of acts heretofore passed in conflict with this act are hereby repealed.

Approved November 5, 1894.

PER CAPITA PAYMENT—$600,000.00.

SEC. 119. The law enacted by the National Council in 1893 session in regard to the $600,000.00 per capita payment is still in force.

Approved November 5, 1894.

DAWES CCMMISSION—RESOLUTION REPLYING TO.

SEC. 120. We still believe that the Government of the United States will prove true to her many pledges and keep perfect faith with our people and will aid instead of obstruct our present form of government to the end that we may enjoy peace and happiness in our sacred home, for which we have paid full compensation.

SEC. 121. We express gratitude to the United States Government for the efforts now being made to suppress all lawlessness in our country, and we hereby pledge all the assistance in our power under the law to bring the offenders to justice.

Approved November 5, 1894.

HARRELL INSTITUTE—REQUIRED TO MAKE REPORT.

SEC. 122. The Harrell Institute or the president thereof shall be notified to comply with terms of contract with the Muskogee Nation, or the Council of the Muskogee Nation will take steps to annull the same. The Principal Chief is hereby instructed to notify the president of that Institute of said action of Council.

Approved November 5, 1894.

STRAY PROPERTY—HOW RECOVERED.

SEC. 123. Any person who shall at any time find his property after the same had been advertised and sold at public sale, shall be required to make satisfactory proof of his title to and ownership thereof; and when he shall furnish such satisfactory proof he shall be entitled to his property, but the same shall not be returned to him until he shall have paid all costs necessarily incurred and paid out by the Nation on account of caring for, posting and selling the same.

SEC. 124. If any person shall have purchased any live stock at any public sale and the owner from whom the same may have strayed shall make proof of his ownership of the property and the same is returned to him, then the person surrendering such property shall, upon an order of the Captain of the Light Horse Company on the National Treasurer, be entitled to receive the amount of money or scrip actually paid by him in the purchase of said property.

Approved November 5, 1894.

STANDS AT GATHERINGS OF CITIZENS.

SEC. 125. From and after the passage of this act it shall

be unlawful for any non-citizen to establish and maintain at or near any place of entertainment or public gathering given by citizens, any stands or other conveniences for the sale, auctioneering or other disposition of any kind of goods, drugs, cider or confectionery without the express consent of the people giving the entertainment, and any violation of this law shall be a sufficient cause for the revocation of any permit under which such offender may be remaining in the country.

Approved November 5, 1894.

DAWES, S. B.—REPORT OF.

SEC. 126. The report made by S. B. Dawes to the Council regarding his work in the prosecution of non-citizens for unlawful introduction of foreign cattle into the Creek country be, and the same is hereby adopted, and the contract made by the Principal Chief of this Nation with said S. B. Dawes, April 7, 1894, for his services as attorney for the Creek Nation for a period of two years from said date, at a salary of fifteen hundred dollars per annum, is hereby ratified.

SEC. 127. The sum of three thousand dollars is hereby approperated, to be paid to said S. B. Dawes by the principal Chief of this Nation, alluding to the terms of said contract for his services as attorney for the Creek Nation for a period of two years from April 7, 1894.

Approved November 5, 1894.

MILE-SQUARE PASTURES—HOLDING STOCK THEREIN PROHIBITED.

SEC. 128. Any citizen of the Muskogee Nation, by blood, adoption, or intermarriage, shall not have the right to introduce any cattle from the Cherokee or Choctaw Nations or any of the States or Territories for the purpose of keeping the same in one mile square pastures.

SEC. 129. Any person violating this act shall be subject

to the fines and penalties imposed by the provisions of the quarantine law, and it shall become the duty of the Judge of the district wherein such violation of this law occurs to direct the Light Horsemen to take down the fences surrounding the same.

Approved November 5, 1894.

OUTLAWS—LIGHT HORSE TO ASSIST UNITED STATES OFFICERS IN ARRESTING.

SEC. 130. The Principal Chief be and is hereby directed to instruct the Judges of each district to order the Light Horse Companies to assist the officers of the United States in capturing or exterminating the bands of outlaws which may be found in our Nation. The Captains of the Light Horse Companies of the several districts are hereby authorized to deputize as many citizens as may be necessary to carry out the purpose of this act.

Approved November 5, 1894.

TREASURER AND AUDITOR TO REPORT WITHIN FOUR DAYS AFTER MEETING OF COUNCIL.

SEC. 131. From and after the passage of this act the National Treasurer and the National Auditor shall submit their reports to the National Council within four days after the meeting thereof in regular session.

SEC. 132. If either of the above named officers shall fail to comply with the requirements of this law, his office shall be deemed to be vacant and the National Council shall proceed at once to elect their successors.

Approved November 5, 1894.

LIGHTHORSEMEN—TO ASSIST U. S. OFFICERS IN APPREHENDING CRIMINALS.

SEC. 133. The act approved November 5, 1894, directing the Principal Chief to instruct the District Judges to authorize their Lighthorsemen to assist U. S. officers in exterminating outlaws, and authorizing Captains of Lighthorse Companies to deputize assistant Lighthorsemen, be and the same is hereby repealed.

Approved January 30, 1895.

MAJORITY—IN ELECTION OF PRINCIPAL CHIEF DEFINED.

SEC. 134. The act of the National Council which became a law by limitation in 1891, regulating the manner of electing the Principal Chief, be and is hereby repealed.

SEC. 135. In all elections of Principal and Second Chiefs, from and after the passage of this act, the word "majority" as appears in Sec. 1, Art. II, of the Constitution of the Muskogee Nation, shall be deemed and taken to have the same significance as the word "plurality," in order that, where more than two candidates shall be voted for, the one receiving a plurality of the votes cast shall be deemed to be legally elected.

Approved January 31, 1895.

PERMIT LAW—AMENDMENT TO.

SEC. 136. The fourth section of the act creating the office of District Inspectors, approved October 30, 1894, be and the same is hereby amended so as to read, "for mechanics one dollar" where it reads "for mechanics one dollar and twenty-five cents."

Approved January 31, 1895.

PERMIT LAW—CORRECTED.

SEC. 137. WHEREAS, there was an error made in the translation and printing of the Permit Law approved October 30, 1894, in section 4, page 11, which reads "non-citizen clerks and accountants in the employ of licensed traders shall be required to pay a monthly tax of fifty (50) cents," is hereby so corrected as to read, "for clerks in the employ of licensed traders, $1.00 per month; for teamsters, gin hands and porters employed by licensed traders, 50 cents per month."

SIX HUNDRED THOUSAND DOLLARS APPROPRIATED.

SEC. 138. There is hereby set apart and appropriated the following sums of money, to-wit: Five hundred thousand dollars ($500,000.00) for the purpose of making a per capita payment to the citizens of the Muskogee Nation; eighty-two thousand dollars ($82,000.00) to be set apart and held subject to such purposes as the regular session of the National Council of October, 1895, may deem proper to make of the same; and eighteen thousand ($18,000.00) to be paid to W. B. Hord and C. W. Turner for services as financial agents when they shall have complied with all the terms and conditions of their employment as provided by act of January 31, 1895.

SEC. 139. The aforesaid sums, aggregating six hundred thousand dollars ($600,000.00) shall be paid out of the proceeds of the sale, transfer and assignment of a portion of the indebtedness of the United States to the Muskogee Nation under act of Congress of March 1, 1889, when the proceeds of such sale, transfer and assignment shall have been paid into the Treasury of the Muskogee Nation as provided for by act of January 31, 1895.

Approved January 31, 1895.

TREASURER TO EXECUTE SPECIAL BOND FOR PAYMENT OF $600,000.00.

SEC. 140. The Treasurer, before receiving any money which may accrue from the sale, transfer and assignment of $600,000.00, a part of the indebtedness of the United States to the Creek Nation, shall be required to execute a good and sufficient bond to the Creek Nation in the penal sum of $600,-000.00 for the faithful distribution and payment of the said

$600,000.00 in accordance with the acts of Council of January 31, 1895.

Approved January 31, 1895.

CENSUS—TO BE TAKEN BY MEMBERS OF COUNCIL.

SEC. 141. As soon as the Principal Chief is notified by the National Treasurer that he has received the proceeds of the sale, transfer and assignment of the six hundred thousand dollars to Street Wykes & Co., he shall set a day and notify the members of the Council to proceed and take a correct census of the citizens and members or their respective towns, and as soon as the census is taken of such town in duplicate, one copy shall be transmitted to the President of the House of Kings, and thereupon the Chief shall call the members of the Council to convene in extra session to compare the census rolls in possession of the members of Council with those transmitted to the President of the House of Kings and shall carefully examine the rolls thoroughly and correct the same, and the payment shall be made according to such corrected rolls. The payment shall be made at Okmulgee, under the rules and regulations as shall be prescribed by the Council.

Approved January 31, 1895.

SIX HUNERED THOUSAND DOLLARS—AUTHORITY TO SELL, TRANSFER AND ASSIGN.

SEC. 142. The act of November 5, 1894, be and is so amended as to read as follows, to-wit:

WHEREAS, By an act of Congress entitled "An Act to ratify and confirm an agreement with the Muskogee Nation of Indians in the Indian Territory, and for other purposes," approved March 1, 1889, the United States of America agreed to, amongst other things, as follows, to-wit:

"In consideration whereof and of the covenant herein

otherwise contained the United States agree to pay to the said Muskogee Nation the sum of ($2,280,857.10) two million two hundred and eighty thousand eight hundred and fifty-seven dollars and ten cents shall be paid to the National Treasurer of said Muskogee Nation or to such other person as shall be duly authorized to receive the same, at such times and in such sums after the due ratification of this agreement (as hereinafter provided) as shall be directed and required by the National Council of said Nation; and the remaining sum of two million dollars shall be set aside apart and remain in the Treasury of the United States to the credit of said Nation and shall bear interest at the rate of five per centum per annum from and after the first day of July, 1889, to be paid to the Treasurer of said Nation and to be judiciously applied under the direction of the legislative Council thereof to the support of their government, the maintenance of schools and educational establishments and such other objects as may be designed to promote the welfare and happiness of the people of the said Muskogee Nation subject to the discretionary direction of the Congress of the United States; *Provided*, That the Congress of the United States may at any time pay over to said Muskogee Nation the whole, or from time to time any part of said principal sum, or of any principal sum belonging to the said Nation held in the Treasury of the United States and thereupon terminate the obligation of the United States in respect thereto and in respect to any further interest upon as much of said principal as shall be so paid and discharged. And further enacted as follows: That the Secretary of the Treasury is hereby authorized and directed to pay out of the appropriation hereby made the sum of two hundred and eighty thousand eight hundred fifty-seven dollars and ten cents to the National Treasurer of said Muskogee Nation or to such person as shall be duly authorized to receive the same at such time and in such sums as shall be directed and required by the National Council of the said Nation. And the Secretary of the Treasury is hereby further authorized and directed to place the remaining two million dollars in the Treasury of the United States to the credit of said Muskogee Nation of Indians to be held for and as provided in said articles of cession and agreement, and to bear interest at the rate of five per centum per annum from and after the first day of July, Anno Domini eighteen hundred and eighty-nine, said interest to be paid to the Treasurer of said Nation annually,'' and

WHEREAS, Not more than ($1,400,000.00) one million four hundred thousand dollars of said money and the interest thereon is needed by said Nation for said purposes; and

WHEREAS, During the past season the country has been visited by a severe drouth, rendering the means of subsistence scarce both within the Nation and the countries bordering thereon, and unless some means are provided to secure the same, many of the people will be subjected to great suffering for want of food during the coming year; and,

WHEREAS, For the purpose of making a per capita payment to the people and to pay outstanding indebtedness of the Nation—

SEC. 143. *Be it Enacted by the National Council of the Muskogee Nation:* That the Congress of the United States be and is hereby requested to authorize the Muskogee Nation to sell, transfer and assign six hundred thousand dollars of said indebtedness, together with the interest to accrue thereon from and after the date of transfer, sale and assignment and to make the principal, six hundred thousand dollars of said indebtedness, payable within not less than five years, nor more than twenty years from the first day of January, 1895.

All acts or parts of acts in conflict with this act are hereby repealed.

Approved January 31, 1895.

FINANCIAL AGENTS—ACT OF EMPLOYMENT.

PREAMBLE.

WHEREAS, By an act of the National Councel of date of January 31, 1895, the Congress of the United States is requested to authorize the Muskogee (or Creek) Nation to sell, transfer and assign $600,000.00 of the indebtedness of the United States to the Muskogee (or Creek) Nation, together with the interest to accure thereon from and after date of transfer, and to make the principal, $600,000.00 of indebtedness, payable within not less than five nor more than twenty years from the first day of January, 1895; and,

WHEREAS, In order to assist and facilitate the proper authorities of the Muskogee (or Creek) Nation in obtaining the consent of Congress so to do, and thereafter in consumating said sale, transfer and assignment of the said indebtedness of $600,000.00 due to the Muskogee (or Creek) Nation of the United States, it is necessary to employ and secure the assistance of a financial agent or agents; therefore,

SEC. 144. That W. B. Hord and C. W. Turner be and they are hereby employed and constituted as the Financial Agents of the Muskogee Nation to assist the proper authorities of the same in obtaining the consent of Congress to make a sale, transfer and assignment of the sum of $600,000.00 of the indebtedness due of the United States to the Muskogee Nation as aforesaid. And when such consent of Congress has been obtained, said W. B. Hord and C. W. Turner are further to assist the proper authorities of the Muskogee Na tion in consumating such sale, transfer and assignment of said sum of $600,000.00 of the indebtedness due as aforesaid from the United States to the Muskogee Nation and secure the payment into the Treasury of the Muskogee Nation the said sum of $600,000.00, proceeds of said sale and assignment, and when said sum shall have been received by the Treasurer of the Muskogee Nation, then W. B. Hord and C. W. Turner shall be paid three per cent. of said $600,000.00 as compensation for their services as Financial Agents of the Muskogee Nation as aforesaid.

SEC. 145. Should no sale, transfer or assignment be made under the provisions of resolution of January 31, 1895, by the assistance of W. B. Hord and C. W. Turner, then in such an event they shall receive no compensation whatever.

Approved January 31, 1895.

SIX HUNDRED THOUSAND DOLLARS—AUTHORIZING L. C. PERRYMAN AND OTHERS TO SELL OR ASSIGN.

PREAMBLE.

WHEREAS, The United States of America, by an act of Congress entitled, "An Act to ratify and confirm an agreement with the Muskogee Nation of Indians in the Indian Territory and for other purposes," approved March 1, 1889, agreed to set apart and place in the Treasury of the United States to the credit of the said Muskogee Nation the sum of $2,000,000.00, bearing interest at the rate of five per centum per annum from and after the first day of July, 1889, and to pay the same to the Treasurer of said Nation, to be judiciously applied under the direction of the legislative Council thereof to the support of their government and maintenance of their schools and educational establishments and such other objects as may be designed to promote the welfare and happiness of the people of the said Muskogee Nation, subject to the discretionary direction of the Congress of the United States; and for the purpose of carrying out the said agreement the sum of $2,000,000.00 was appropriated; and the Secretary of the Treasury was authorized and directed to place the sum of $2,000,000.00 in the Treasury of the United States to the credit of said Nation, to be held for and as provided in said articles of agreement, to bear interest at the rate of five per centum per annum from and after the first day of July, 1889, said interest to be paid to the Treasurer of said Nation annually; and

WHEREAS, Not more than $1,400,000.00 and the interest thereon is needed for the support of the Government, the maintenance of schools and educational establishments, or other purposes, and the people of said Nation desire a per capita payment; and

WHEREAS, An act of the National Council of January 31, 1895, asking the consent of Congress of the United States to sell, transfer and assign six hundred thousand dollars of said indebtedness, together with the interest to accrue thereon from and after the date of transfer, sale and assignment, and to make the principal, $600,000.00, of said indebtedness payable within not less than five years nor more than twenty years from the first day of January, 1895; and

WHEREAS, Messrs. Street Wykes & Co., of New York City, have submitted a proposition in writing to purchase $600,000.00 of said indebtedness, together with the interest thereon at the rate of five per centum per annum from and after the date of transfer, and to pay therefor the sum of $600,000.00 in lawful money of the United States, now, therefore,

SEC. 146. That Leguest C. Perryman, Principal Chief Muskogee Nation, and Samuel Grayson, Treasurer Muskogee Nation, are hereby authorized and directed to make, execute and deliver to Messrs. Street Wykes & Co., of New York City, or their assigns, a legal sale, transfer and assignment of $600,000.00 of the indebtedness which the United States of America agreed to pay the Muskogee Nation in pursuance of an act of Congress entitled, "An act to ratify and confirm an agreement with the Muskogee Nation of Indians in the Indian Territory, and for other purposes," approved March 1, 1889, together with the interest thereon at the rate of five per centum per annum from and after the date of transfer, upon the payment by Messrs. Street Wykes & Co. of six hundred thousand dollars in lawful money of the United States of America to the Treasurer of the Muskogee Nation; *Provided*, the Congress of the United States of America authorize the sale, transfer and assignment of such indebtedness and the payment of the principal within not less than five years nor more than twenty years from the first day of January, 1895, together with the annual interest thereon as it becomes due.

Approved January 30, 1895.

COMMITTEE OF EIGHTEEN—APPOINTMENT OF

SEC. 147. That a special committee, to be composed of six members from the House of Kings and twelve members from the House of Warriors, be appointed to take charge of the census rolls of the various towns and carefully examine the same and ascertain whether or not they are correct, and if any of them are found to contain the names of non-citizens all such names shall be expunged from the rolls and reported separately to the National Council. All the acts of the special committee herein provided for shall be subject to the approval of the National Council.

Approved May 15, 1895.

PER CAPITA PAYMENT—WHO ARE ENTITLED TO PARTICIPATE IN.

WHEREAS, It has become notorious that by questionable and unjust methods and practices many non-citizens have heretofore been counted as citizens and participated in the per capita distribution of the public funds of the Nation; and,

WHEREAS, Such persons as have in this manner obtained a share in the payments of moneys of the Nation made to her citizens, claim that by such participation they have become fully recognized citizens thereof, entitled to all the rights, privileges and immunities incident thereto, which claim, if admitted, must eventuate in great injustice to bona fide citizens of the Nation; therefore,

SEC. 148. The fact alone that any person has at any time participated in the per capita distribution of any of the public moneys of the Muskogee Nation does not make of such a person a citizen of the Muskogee Nation, entitled to the rights and privileges of recognized citizens thereof, and shall not by any authority of the Nation be accepted or construed as evidence sufficiently perfecting and establishing such claim.

SEC. 149. The committee of eighteen (18), appointed by act of the extraordinary session of Council approved May 15, 1895, to examine and correct the census rolls of 1895, are hereby instructed and directed to entertain and consider any and all challenges and questions urged in good faith by any respectable citizen against the claim of any person to citizenship in this Nation, and strike from the rolls and preserve a correct list of all the names so stricken out and report the same to the present session of Council.

SEC. 150. All persons of Creek blood and all adopted citizens of any blood who reside in the Muskogee Nation, and whose citizenship is not questioned, are hereby declared entititled to participate in the coming per capita payment.

SEC. 151. All persons residing in the surrounding Nations, whether Creek by blood or otherwise, who claim Creek citizenship, but have been recognized as citizens by the authorities of the Nation in which they reside, are hereby debarred from participation in said per capita payment.

Approved May 17, 1895.

CITIZENSHIP COMMISSION.

PREAMBLE.

WHEREAS, The opinion prevails throughout the country that a large number of non-citizens have been enrolled as citizens on the different census rolls that have been made from time to time in the past; and,

WHEREAS, It is curently asserted, and believed by many, that a large number of claimants who have heretofore appeared before the committees of the National Council on citizenship and other authorities of the Nation and established or obtained recognition of their claim to citizenship in the Nation, accomplished the same by the undue use of money and other fraudulent means; and,

WHEREAS, In all former actions involving the question of the citizenship of any person in the Muskogee Nation this Nation had no representative to appear as attorney to defend her interests in that behalf; therefore,

SEC. 152 That a commission, to be styled "The Citizenship Commission," to be composed of five (5) of the most competent citizens of this Nation be and is hereby created, whose duty it shall be to sit as a high court and try, determine and settle all and only such causes as shall involve the question of the right of citizenship of any person in the Muskogee Nation that shall be presented to it, either by claimant or the duly authorized representative of the Nation, as hereinafter provided.

The members of the Commission shall be elected by the present session of the Council, and shall meet as soon as practicable after their appointment and organize by electing one of their number President and employing one competent interpreter and two (2) well qualified clerks. One clerk shall take charge of all census rolls submitted to the Commission, read and compare them with other collatteral matter that shall be presented for that purpose, and shall keep a list of all such matters and documents, and stand responsible for their due preservation. One of the clerks shall preserve a docket and number of all cases and carefully and correctly record all such testimony of witnesses as the Commission shall deem worthy of record; shall carefully and correctly and in due form record all findings of facts and decisions of the Commission, issue all subpœnas, summons and calls for persons or papers ordered by it. When organized as provided, the Commission shall give public notice through all the newspapers published in the Nation of the time and place of its meeting at least thirty (30) days previous to such meeting. Its sessions shall be held in the Council house at Okmulgee, the first of which shall be on the second Tuesday of July, 1895. They may adjourn and meet from time to time, as the interests of their business may seem to warrant, and the presence of a majority shall be sufficient for the lawful transaction of business. They shall have full authority to summon witnesses and call for persons and papers and do all other things necessary and proper to show all the facts in any case that may come before it, and in summoning witnesses the process shall be by notifying the Judges of the several Districts, when he shall in turn subpœna the witnesses desired through their lighthorsemen. All witnesses subpœnaed on part of the Nation shall be paid by the Nation the same per diem and mileage as paid to witnesses appearing before the District Courts in criminal cases; and the Commission shall issue certificates of indebtedness, attested by the signatures of the President and recording clerk, and the National Council, at its next regular session, make appropriation to cover such witness fees.

SEC. 153. All persons who shall appear before the Commission claiming citizenship in the Muskogee Nation, and all others whose names now appear as citizens on any of the census rolls taken at any time, or on any of the public records of the Nation, the validity of whose citizenship shall in good faith be questioned by any responsible citizen, shall be plaintiffs and entitled to the right of council and to all other rights usual and incident to the trial of a cause in a court of justice in this Nation. They shall file written allegations before the commission, setting forth clearly the grounds of their claim and the names of the witnesses they desire to have subpœnaed in their behalf, and shall file a bond satisfactory to the President of the Commission that they will themselves pay their witnesses the same per diem and mileage as paid to witnesses on part of the Nation. And when such allegations and witness bond are properly filed, then the Commission shall subpœna the witnesses for the claimant in the same manner as witnesses for the Nation are subpœnaed; and if any witness, being a Muskogee citizen, shall refuse to obey any subpœna of the Commission or to appear before it when duly summoned, except in case of sickness or other unavoidable hindrance, he shall be fined twenty-five ($25.00) dollars, and no property except improvements, house furniture, and wearing apparel shall be exempt from seizure and forced sale to satisfy said fine. The President of the Commission shall have authority to administer oath, and any witness testifying falsely under oath shall be subject to the same pains and penalties prescribed by Muskogee law for the crime of perjury; and when the attorney for the Nation shall become satisfied that any citizen has sworn falsely in any cause before the Commission he shall promptly report the same to the District Attorney of Okmulgee District, together with such facts as he may have to justify criminal proceedings, and the District Attorney shall, without unnecessary delay, proceed to arraign and try the accused in the court of his District for the crime of perjury.

SEC. 154. In the examination and adjudication of the

claims of negroes to citizenship in the Muskogee Nation the provisions of the treaty of 1866 with the United States shall govern, and the subsequent acts of adoption passed by the National Council shall govern, and in cases of claim to citizenship by reason of Indian blood the act of the National Council as appears in sections 295 to 298, inclusive, of the Muskogee laws, edition 1893, shall govern; and when any case shall be decided in favor of any person by the Commission the plaintiff shall ever afterwards be a full citizen and accorded all the rights of any other citizen. And in any enumeration hereafter to be made of the citizens of the Nation, any person applying for registration, against whose citizenship any question may arise, shall be required to trace his or her origin to the rolls of the names of citizens to be prepared under this act.

SEC. 155. The Principal Chief shall nominate, with the five Commissioners herein provided for, one competent attorney, who shall be well versed in the treaties, compacts and laws of the Muskogee Nation, who shall be confirmed by the Council. His duty shall be to defend the Nation in all cases of claims to citizenship therein which may be filed before the Commission, to the end that no fraudulent claims may be passed by said tribunal. He shall diligently inquire into all cases of suspected fraud in the enrollment of citizens at any time; and if he shall have cause to believe that any person whose name appears on any census roll of any alleged citizens of the Nation, or that any person has heretofore proved his or her rights through fraudulent means, he shall give them due notice and shall move that their names be stricken from the rolls until they re-establish their rights through competent testimony to the satisfaction of the Commission. All cases before this tribunal shall be decided by vote, and a majority vote shall stand and be the final decision of that body. All points of law contested before the

Commission shall be decided in like manner and have the same force and effect as if decided by any other competent court.

SEC. 156. Each commissioner, enterpreter, clerk and the attorney for the Nation shall receive a per diem of four ($4.00) dollars during the time they are engaged in the business herein prescribed, together with mileage at the rate of 10 cents per mile in going to and returning from their sessions.

SEC. 157. That two thousand and five hundred($2,500.00) dollars, or so much thereof as may be necessary, be, and is hereby appropriated for the payment of per diem and mileage of members, interpreter and clerks of the Commission, to be issued in warrants by the Principal Chief upon certificates issued by the President of the Commission.

Approved May 30, 1895.

TWO HUNDRED THOUSAND DOLLARS—TO BE PAID OUT PER CAPITA.

SEC. 158. That the sum of two hundred thousand dollars, which has been appropriated by the Congress of the United States and placed to the credit of the Creek Nation in the sub-treasury at St. Louis, be, and the same is hereby set apart for the purpose of making a per capita payment to the citizens of the Muskogee Nation.

SEC. 159. That the National Treasurer of the Muskogee Nation be, and is hereby authorized and directed to make the disbursement of the per capita payment to the citizens of the Muskogee Nation at the capitol building.

SEC. 160. The National Treasurer, before receiving any money for the purpose of making a per capita payment, shall be required to execute a good and sufficient bond (nobody but citizens of the Creek Nation shall be accepted as such bondsmen) in the penal sum of two hundred thousand dollars for the faithful distribution and payment of the said $200,000.00 in accordance with the acts of Council of May, 1895.

SEC. 161. The date for making payment shall be fixed by the Treasurer, of which he shall notify the King or Warriors of each town as soon as the necessary pay-roll shall have been completed therefor.

SEC. 162. The Treasurer shall employ such clerical assistance as he may deem necessary to properly disburse the two hundred thousand dollars, and he shall pay such assistants four ($4.00) dollars per day; he shall also have authority to call on two Lighthorsemen from each of the six Districts to act as guards, and he shall pay the actual lodging and boarding expenses of such Lighthorsemen during their service in such capacity.

SEC. 163. That the sum of two hundred thousand dollars be, and is hereby appropriated and set apart for the purpose of making a per capita payment to the citizens of the Muskogee Nation.

SEC. 164. That the sum of four thousand and five hundred dollars, or so much thereof as may be necessary, be, and is hereby appropriated out of the general fund and set apart and used for defraying the expenses of making the payment of two hundred thousand dollars per capita payment.

SEC. 165. The National Treasurer shall issue a certificate to each person the amount due him for services rendered as assistant during the payment, and on presentation of the certificates to the Principal Chief he shall issue a draft to cover the same and shall report all certificates so paid to the National Council of 1895.

SEC. 166. Should any person or persons not being able to come and draw his or her money, giving satisfactory proof to the Treasurer, his or her money can be drawn out by the

Council members of their respective towns and shall be required to receipt for the same.

SEC. 167. The Treasurer shall render to the next regular session of Council a full report of all the work herein provided for.

SEC. 168. That the treasurer be, and he is hereby, authorized and directed to use what surplus fund may occur by odd cents from the division out of the said $200,000.00 per capita payment, set apart for the purpose of making a per capita payment, to pay express charges bringing money from St. Louis to Creek Nation, and he shall be required to make a report, with the receipts from the express agent, showing the amount paid by him, to the National Council of 1895.

Approved June 1, 1895.

TWO HUNDRED THOUSAND DOLLARS—READY FOR PAYMENT PER CAPITA.

SEC. 169. *Be it Resolved by the National Council of the Muskogee Nation:* That the sum of six thousand dollars out of the $200,000.00 being illegally paid to said Turner and Hord, financial agents, by the Treasurer of the Muskogee Nation, and that the said sum of six thousand dollars being refunded to the Creek Nation in cash or check by the Treasurer of the Muskogee Nation, which money is at C. W. Turner's, at Muskogee, I. T., ready for disbursement of the per capita payment to the citizens of the Muskogee Nation.

SEC. 170. *Be it further Resolved:* That the sum of one hundred and ninety-four thousand dollars in the sub-treasury at St. Louis and the said six thousand dollars, being refunded in cash or check by the Treasurer of the Muskogee Nation, is at C. W. Turner's, at Muskogee, I. T., making a total amount of two hundred thousand dollars, ready for the distribution of the per capita payment to the citizens of the Muskogee Nation.

Approved June 3, 1895.

WARRANT COMMITTEE—APPOINTED.

SEC. 171. *Be it Resolved by the National Council of the Muskogee Nation:* That a committee of three competent persons be elected by the National Council, whose duty shall be to call for and receive all outstanding National warrants and carefully examine and register the same, noting the number, amount and purpose for which issued, and ascertain whether or not any warrant has been duplicated, and no warrant shall be cashed by the Treasurer until it has been examined and approved of. If any duplicate warrants are discovered by the committee they shall retain the same and report them to the next session of the National Council.

SEC. 172. *Be it further Resolved:* That each member of the committee shall, while in actual service, receive the same per diem as members of the National Council, and upon certificate of the Chairman thereof the Principal Chief shall issue warrants to them.

SEC. 173. *Be it Enacted by the National Council:* That a sum sufficient to cover their per diem is hereby appropriated.

Approved June 5, 1895.

CENSUS—COMMITTEE REPORT ON.

SEC. 174. OKMULGEE, I. T., June 8, 1895.

Hon. National Council, M. N.:

GENTLEMEN:—We, your committee of eighteen, appointed to consider and correct the census rolls of the several towns, as handed in by the Town Chiefs, have examined and corrected the forty-seven rolls.

The aggregate number on the rolls is 13,841.

The number enrolled which were stricken from the rolls by the committee as doubtful is 619.

Having completed the work assigned us, we submit this report and asking that the report be adopted and committee discharged.

Respectfully,

M. J. Smith, Chairman.

Mildred McIntosh, Clerk.

Approved June 8, 1895.

COUNCIL MEMBERS—APPORTIONMENT OF.

Sec. 175. Each town of the Muskogee Nation is hereby required and instructed to base its next general election in September, 1895, for members of the National Council, upon the number of citizens as shown by the census reported by the committee of eighteen to the Council on June 8, 1895, which is to say, for—

NO. TOWN NAME.	CITIZENS.	K.	W.
1—Coweta	558	1	3
2—Tuckabache	793	1	4
3—Cussehta	441	1	3
4—Euchee	590	1	3
5—Tuskegee	421	1	3
6—Broken Arrow	349	1	2
7—L. R. Tulsa	380	1	2
8—Oeogufkee	240	1	2
9—Kechopatake	306	1	2
10—Thlopthlocco	309	1	2
11—Hickory Ground	343	1	2
12—Eufaula, Candn	244	1	2
13—Kialigee	219	1	2
14—Nuyarker	208	1	2
15—Lockapoka	214	1	2
16—Thlewahle	199	1	1
17—Tulsa, Candn	163	1	1
18—Arpehka, N. F.	125	1	1
19—Green Leaf	114	1	1
20—Fish Pond	163	1	1
21—Cheyarha	165	1	1
22—Hitchetee	196	1	1

23—Lukontulahassee	105	1	1
24—Hellabe	105	1	1
25—Artussee	145	1	1
26—Alabama	166	1	1
27—Big Spring	188	1	1
28—Eufaula, D. F.	137	1	1
29—Quassarte, No. 1	76	1	1
30—Quassarte, No. 2	46	1	1
31—Tokpafka	83	1	1
32—Arbekochee	98	1	1
33—Tulwathlocco	164	1	1
34—Okfuske, Candn.	116	1	1
35—Concharte	189	1	1
36—Wewoka	87	1	1
37—Okchiye	183	1	1
38—Tulahassochee	58	1	1
39—Okfuske, D. F.	85	1	1
40—Hutchchuppa	187	1	1
41—Tulmochussee	94	1	1
42—Arpehka, D. F.	127	1	1
43—Osochee	75	1	1
44—Tuladegee	139	1	1
45—Arkansas, colored	1934	1	10
46—Canadian, colored	1440	1	8
47—North Fork, colored	1029	1	6

—until some further enumeration shall necessitate a different apportionment.

Approved June 8, 1895.

MILEAGE—WITNESSES' AND JURORS', REDUCED.

SEC. 176. From and after the passage of this act the mileage of jurors and witnesses attending the District Courts in criminal cases is hereby reduced to five cents per mile each way.

All acts and parts of acts in conflict herewith are hereby repealed.

Approved October 15, 1895.

PER CAPITA PAYMENT—$400,000.00.

SEC. 177. The sum of four hundred thousand dollars of the remaining $1,800,000.00 derived from the sale of

Oklahoma lands, now standing to the credit of the Muskogee Nation in the United States Treasury, shall be withdrawn—one hundred thousand thereof to be expended in payment of our national indebtedness, and three hundred thousand dollars to be distributed per capita to the citizens of the Muskogee Nation.

SEC. 178. The acting Principal Chief is hereby authorized and directed, for and in behalf of the Muskogee Nation to make requisition upon the proper authorities of the United States, in such forms as may be required by the said authorities for the payment to our National Treasurer of the Muskogee Nation of the sum of four hundred thousand dollars, out of the moneys specified in the foregoing section.

SEC. 179. Our National Delegates, who shall be accredited to represent our Nation in Washington the ensuing session of Congress, are hereby authorized and directed to act as the financial agents (in connection with their other duties) of the Muskogee Nation in securing for the said Nation the sum of four hundred thousand dollars from the U. S. Government, for which service they shall not receive any additional compensation, nor shall employ assistance in the discharge of this duty upon the promise of any fee to be paid out of any funds belonging to said Nation.

SEC. 180. All acts or parts of acts in conflict with the provisions of this act are hereby repealed.

Approved November 21, 1895.

DISTRICT INSPECTOR—ACT DEFINING DUTY OF, AMENDED.

SEC. 181. That the act entitled, "An Act Creating Office of District Inspectors," approved October 30, 1894, be, and the same is hereby amended in the following manner, to-wit: Strike out that portion of Section 4 beginning with the words, "The tax for common laborers," etc., and ending with the words, "monthly tax of fifty (50) cents," and substitute therefor the following words, to-wit: "The tax on common laborers, renters or tenants on farms, or on clerks or other employes of licensed traders shall be fifty (50) cents per month, and the tax on mechanics, otherwise than as provided for by the licensed tax law, shall be one ($1.00) dollar per month."

Approved November 26, 1895.

LARCENY—CONCEALMENT OF IDENTITY OF ANIMAL KILLED DECLARED TO BE.

Sec. 182. Should any person or persons be found in possession of a hog that has been recently killed, with its head cut off or its ears recently mutilated in a manner so as to disfigure the ear mark of such hog; or should any person be found in possession of the carcass of a beef that shall appear evident to have been recently killed, and should such person fail or refuse to produce or show the hide of such beef, in good order, for inspection by any person who may demand it, such person or persons shall be deemed and held guilty of the crime of larceny, and upon conviction shall suffer the same penalty as provided for by the law governing larceny.

Sec. 183. Should any person find any other person in possession of any hog or hogs or beef or part of a beef, as described in the preceding section, it shall be the duty of such person to at once report the matter to the nearest Lighthorseman, and in case a Lighthorseman cannot be found at once, then it shall be the duty of such person to call to his aid any person or number of persons he may deem necessary and to proceed at once to examine such hog or hogs or beef or part of a beef, and if, upon examination, the facts ascertained shall be deemed sufficient to secure a conviction, then such person shall report the same to the Prosecuting Attorney of the District in which the crime has been committed.

SEC. 184. When a conviction shall have been secured for the violation of the above law, and the rightful owner of such hog or hogs or beef cannot be ascertained, the value of the hog, hogs or beef shall be fixed by the Court and the Court shall order the Lighthorsemen to proceed and collect the value as fixed by the Court from the person so convicted and turn the amount over to the witness or witnesses that caused such conviction.

Approved November 26, 1895.

BOND—OF PRISONERS, AMENDED.

SEC. 185. That Sec. 140, page 54, Creek Laws, edition of 1893, be so amended that the words "within twenty days" be stricken out and the words "within five days" substituted therefor.

Approved November 29, 1895.

NAMES OF CHILDREN UNBORN TO BE ERASED FROM CENSUS ROLLS.

SEC. 186. *Be it Resolved by the National Council of the Muskogee Nation*: That, as there appears to have been enrolled some names of children yet unborn, the members of the different towns are required to erase all such names from their respective census rolls.

Approved November 30, 1895.

WARRANTS—CERTAIN, ISSUED BY L. C. PERRYMAN, DECLARED TO BE VOID.

SEC. 187. *Be it Enacted by the National Council of the Muskogee Nation:* That all warrants issued by L. C. Perryman after his suspension from office by this body, or since June, 1895, shall be null and void and of no account, and the Treasurer is hereby directed that he shall not pay any of the above-named warrants.

Approved December 4, 1895.

OMITTED NAMES AND NAMES OF CHILDREN.

SEC. 188. *Be it Resolved by the Conference Committee of the National Council:* That all children that were born between the dates of June 8 and September 24, 1895, and also all citizens who were omitted from the census rolls last taken are hereby entitled to participate in the present per capita payment.

Approved December 4, 1895.

WARRANTS—NOS. 8250 TO 8291, AND NOS. 8291 TO 8316 NOT TO BE PAID.

SEC. 189. *Be it Resolved by the National Council of the Muskogee Nation:* That the National Treasurer is hereby notified and directed to not pay warrants numbered 8250 to 8291 and also 8291 to 8316, but shall, if possible, ascertain by whom they were issued and to whom issued and report the same to the Principal Chief.

Approved December 13, 1895.

FOUR HUNDRED THOUSAND DOLLARS TO BE CONVERTED INTO BONDS.

SEC. 190. That the Congress of the United States be, and is hereby requested to authorize the Muskogee Nation to sell, transfer and assign $400,000.00 of the proceeds of the sale of Oklahoma, now invested with the United States Government, together with the interest to accrue thereon from January 1, 1896, and to make said principal, $400,000.00, payable within not less than twenty years from said date of January 1, 1896.

SEC. 191. That the said delegates be, and are hereby authorized, empowered and directed to do everything that may be necessary to be done by the Muskogee Nation to carry into effect the provisions of Section 1 of this act, to make the necessary transfer and assignment for the Muskogee Nation, and have the money placed to the credit of the Muskogee Nation subject to its orders, and any and all acts of said delegates as herein authorized shall be taken, and is hereby declared to be the authority of the Muskogee Nation.

Approved December 13, 1895.

THREE THOUSAND DOLLARS—APPROPRIATED FOR REMOVAL OF INTRUDERS.

SEC. 192. All non-citizens residing in the limits of the Muskogee Nation not in accordance with XV Article, treaty of 1856, and permit law of the Muskogee Nation, are hereby declared to be intruders, and the Principal Chief be, and is hereby authorized and instructed to use all means, by and with the assistance of the United States Indian Agent, to eject all such intruders from within the limits of the Muskogee Nation.

SEC. 193. The District Inspector shall furnish to the Principal Chief the names of persons, and their occupations, who are residents of their respective Districts contrary to treaty stipulations and to the permit law of the Muskogee Nation.

SEC. 194. That the sum of three thousand ($3,000.00) dollars be, and is hereby appropriated and placed at the disposal of the Principal Chief, who is required to make an itemized report of the disposition of said sum to the October term of the National Council, 1896. The Principal Chief is hereby authorized to issue warrant or warrants to the amount not greater than one thousand ($1,000.00) dollars of the above said sum of money, and after such expenditure is made, then in his judgment necessary to issue warrant or warrants of the balance of said appropriation, he may do so for the purpose of carrying the foregoing acts into effect.

Approved December 18, 1895.

CITIZENSHIP COMMISSION—LAW ON AMENDED.

SEC. 195. That the act creating the Citizenship Commission, found on page 6 of the Acts and Resolutions of the Creek Council of 1895, be so amended as to read: "They shall have authority to summon witnesses and call for persons and papers and do all other things necessary and proper to show all the facts in any case that may come before it."

SEC. 196. It shall be the duty of the Commission to employ two citizens of the Muskogee Nation to act as Light Horsemen or Messengers of said court, and for their services they shall receive $2.00 per day during actual service. They shall be sworn in by the president of said court and commissioned by the Principal Chief.

SEC. 197. The Citizenship Commission shall complete its work by September 30, 1896.

Approved August 7, 1896.

CITIZENSHIP COMMISSION—LAW ON REPEALED.

SEC. 198. That so much of the law creating and defining the duties of the Commission on Citizenship as authorize said Commission to receive, investigate and determine the rights of applicants for citizenship, be and is hereby repealed, and said Commission is hereby estopped from passing upon any more applications for citizenship.

SEC. 199. Nothing herein contained shall be construed to interfere with or in any way modify the rights of said Commission under the law to examine the census rolls as corrected and submitted to it by the members of Council, under an act of the National Council approved August 10, 1896.

SEC. 200. That the Commission on Citizenship be further continued in office with full authority to act as specially directed in section second of this act and shall so continue until their work is completed.

Approved October 14, 1896.

ROLY MCINTOSH, Acting Prin. Chief.

CRIMINAL COURTS—SESSION OF.

SEC. 201. That the law found on pages 6 and 7, pamphlet law book, edition of 1894, regulating the time for holding criminal court in the several districts, be and the same is hereby repealed; and the judges of the several districts shall hold criminal court whenever a sufficient number of indictments has been made to, in his judgment, justify the convening of the court.

Approved October 20, 1896.

SUPREME COURT—INTERPRETER OF.

SEC. 202. The Supreme Court of the Nation is hereby authorized to employ a competent Interpreter, who is conversant with both the Creek and English languages and able to translate from English to Creek or from Creek to English, whose pay shall be the same as the clerk of the court.

Approved October 20, 1896.

PARDON—THIRD OFFENSE LARCENY.

SEC. 203. Every person who has been convicted of the third offense of larceny and has been pardoned by the Chief shall be considered and held to have been pardoned for both the preceding offenses, and should he again be convicted of the same offense he shall receive the penalty of fifty lashes upon the bare back, as though he had never before been convicted and punished for the same offense.

Approved October 29, 1896.

DANCE HALL—NOT ALLOWED.

SEC. 204. No person or persons shall be allowed to run a public dance hall within one-half mile of the Capitol building. This act shall be subject to the pains and penalties prescribed in section 158, found on page 61, edition 1893.

Approved October 28, 1896.

SESSIONS OF COUNCIL.

SEC. 205. From and after the passage of this act, the next two regular sessions of the National Council shall each consist of fifteen (15) working days, and the third session of thirty (30) working days; the same rule to govern in all succeeding sessions.

Approved October 30, 1896.

DU VAL, BEN T.—SALARY.

SEC. 206. That the sum of two thousand nine hundred ($2,900.00) dollars be and is hereby appropriated to be placed in the hands of the Principal Chief to be by him used in paying Ben T. DuVal for services rendered in preparing rebuttal evidence to be presented to the Dawes Commission in answer to evidence presented to said Commission by applicants for citizenship in the Creek Nation; for services rendered in presenting arguments before the Dawes Commission in behalf of the Nation on September 12th last, and also for services to be rendered in appealed cases decided against the Nation by the Dawes Commission or the Creek court on citizenship, and in resisting cases appealed from the decision of the Dawes Commission or the Creek Commission on Citizenship by applicants for citizenship.

SEC. 207. The Principal Chief is hereby specially authorized and directed to see that the said DuVal faithfully performs his duties as attorney for the Nation and uses every lawful and proper means necessary to successfully defeat all applicants for citizenship whose cases may be appealed to the U. S. Court by the Nation or who may themselves appeal to the U. S. Court from the decision of the Dawes Commission or the Creek Commission on Citizenship.

SEC. 208. The Principal Chief shall issue the appropriation hereinabove provided for to the said DuVal in three separate installments as his work shall progress and the cases shall be accordingly disposed of, and the said DuVal shall pay all court fees and other incidental expenses of any nature whatsoever out of said appropriation as the same shall be paid to him as herein directed, and the said appropriation of two thousand nine hundred ($2,900.00) dollars shall be a full and complete settlement of all accounts for services heretofore rendered or to be hereafter rendered by said DuVal in all matters pertaining to applicants for citizenship in the Creek Nation.

SEC. 209. All acts or parts of acts in conflict with any of the provisions of this act are hereby repealed.

Became a law by limitation November 2, 1896.

PER CAPITA—$400,000.00, AND CREEK DELEGATION.

PREAMBLE.

WHEREAS, In consequence of an almost unprecedented drought in the Indian Territory, the principal crops of the Nation have, in an extensive portion of the country, been almost a complete failure, by which much hardship is already being entailed on the Muskogee or Creek Nation and which suffering will become greater as the winter months come on, rendering it imperative that precautionary measures for relief of the people be adopted by our government, and

WHEREAS, The public debt of the Nation has become burdensome, demanding that more vigorous and definite measures be taken providing for the early redemption of the national obligations now outstanding against our treasury, therefore

SEC. 210. That so much of the act of December 13, 1895, as makes an appropriation of $400,000.00 of the purchase money received for the Oklahoma lands, be and the same is hereby re-enacted and reaffirmed; and $200,000.00 thereof shall be used in payment on the outstanding indebtedness of the Nation, and the remaining $200,000.00 shall be paid in equal shares *per capita* to all *bona fide* citizens of the Nation at as early a day as practicable.

SEC. 211. The present session of Council shall appoint two delegates whose duty shall be to proceed to Washington, D. C., and use all power and means delegated to them, calling to their aid if necessary the influence and co-operation of the commissioners provided by the present Council; and if possible and proper, that also of the body known as the Dawes Commission, for the purpose of securing the early payment by the government of the four hundred thousand ($400,000.00) dollars hereinbefore appropriated.

SEC. 212. That the Principal Chief be and is hereby authorized and directed for and on behalf of the Muskogee Nation to make requisition upon the proper authorities of the United States in such forms as may be required by such authorities, for the payment and placing to the credit of the Muskogee Nation in the subtreasury of the United States at St. Louis, of the sum of $400,000.00, the same being a part of the purchase money received for the Oklahoma lands, the cession of which to the United States was completed January 19, 1889. And the requisition when made shall be taken and accepted as, and is hereby declared to be the requisition of the proper authorities of the Muskogee Nation.

SEC. 213. The delegates herein provided for shall be, and act as, ex-officio members of the commission of five (5) appointed to meet the Dawes Commission, with the powers and privileges of the said commission.

SEC. 214. The national delegates herein provided for shall each be paid, for his services, in national warrants to be preferred over and above others, the sum of nine hundred and twenty-four ($924.00) dollars, and two hundred (200.00) dollars each for the expenses of travel; the further sum of five hundred ($500.00) dollars is hereby appropriated for defraying such necessary incidental expenses as shall arise in the course of the business of said delegates, whose term of service as delegates to Washington shall commence on the 20th day of November, 1896, and end the 1st day of April, 1897.

Approved November 2, 1896.

ROLY MCINTOSH, Acting Prin. Chief.

WALNUT TIMBER—AUTHORITY TO SELL.

SEC. 215. That the judges of the several districts be and they are hereby authorized and directed to take charge of walnut timber cut down unlawfully in their respective districts and enter into contracts with responsible parties and have such timber hauled and shipped to market.

SEC. 216. The district judges shall sell such timber for not less than seven ($7.00) dollars per thousand feet for first-class timber, five ($5.00) dollars per thousand for second class and three ($3.00) dollars for third class, over and above all expenses, and these several amounts of royalty shall be paid to the district judges before the timber is shipped from the Nation.

SEC. 217. The district judges shall report on the first day of each month to the national treasurer the amount of timber shipped and also transmit at the same time the amount of royalty collected during the preceding month, and the present bond of the district judges shall stand good for the faithful performance of the duties herein imposed.

SEC. 218. As soon as all of the down timber is disposed of as herein provided for this act shall cease and be of no further force or effect.

Approved November 3, 1896.

ROYALTY ON BORDER PASTURES.

SEC. 219. The owners of contract pastures shall, after the passage of this law, be required to pay two-thirds of the royalty due the Nation in cash, the same to be passed to the credit of the school funds of the Nation.

Approved November 6, 1896.

SEC. 220. The National Treasurer shall pay to such citizens as may be entitled thereto one-half of the royalties on oil, gas, coal, and other minerals which shall have been paid to the Muskogee Nation in accordance with the provisions of an act approved December 3, 1887, providing for the mining of coal in the Muskogee Nation, and "An Act Amendatory to the Coal Law," approved November 5, 1894, which shall have been derived from mines or wells located upon the land legally held by such citizen or citizens. The amount of such royalties to be determined from the reports of the national weigher.

SEC. 221. In the event two or more citizens shall claim the right of possession to a parcel of land upon which the royalties have been paid as aforesaid, the national treasurer shall retain the royalties derived from such land until the right of possession thereto has been determined.

SEC. 222. Nothing herein shall be construed as allowing any company owning larger than one mile square pasture any royalty as hereinabove provided for.

Approved November 7, 1896.

PERMIT—TO NON-CITIZEN PROHIBITED.

SEC. 223. From and after the passage of this act, no permit shall be issued to any non-citizen to reside within the Muskogee Nation for any purpose whatever, except those permitted as herein after provided.

SEC. 224. Any citizen of this Nation who shall permit or allow any non-citizen to work upon his (the citizen's) farm or premises after the date of January 1, 1897 shall be guilty of misdemeanor.

SEC. 225. Any citizen of this Nation who shall employ

or work any non-citizen within the Muskogee Nation in any manner and in any kind of work whatever, after the 1st day of January, 1897, shall be guilty of a misdemeanor.

SEC. 226. It is hereby made the duty of the prosecuting attorneys of the several districts to indict and prosecute all offenders against the provisions of this act in their respective districts, and all persons duly convicted for a violation of any of the provisions of this act shall be fined in a sum not less than fifty ($50.00) dollars nor more than one hundred ($100.00) dollars for each offense, at the discretion of the court, and upon failure to pay such fines as the court may fix, then he, the convicted party, shall be punished by whipping fifty lashes upon the bare back.

SEC. 227. The provisions of this act shall not apply to physicians, surgeons, licensed traders, teachers, preachers and missionaries of any denomination; provided, however, that they shall not have nor exercise the right of employing and working within the limits of the Muskogee Nation any non-citizens common laborers; and

SEC. 228. All contracts that were made between our citizens and non-citizens for the present year ending December 31, 1896, shall be considered as valid and all persons holding permits and laboring under contracts made by our citizens, shall be allowed to remain within the Muskogee Nation during the continuance of their contracts; provided, such contracts shall expire December 31, 1896.

SEC. 229. Any citizen of this Nation who shall, after passage of this act, contract with any non-citizen to remain and work within the Muskogee Nation after January 1st, 1897, shall be considered as having violated the provisions of this act and shall be subject to all the pains and penalties prescribed herein for violation of same; and

SEC. 230. Any judge or prosecuting attorney who shall fail to execute the provisions of this act shall be subject to impeachment and removal from office for a neglect of duty.

Approved November 6, 1896.

SUPERINTENDENT OF PUBLIC INSTRUCTION.

SEC. 231. That the law creating the Board of Education defining their duties, found on pages 31, 32 and 33, inclusive, and embraced in sections 52 to 64, inclusive, revised edition Creek Laws of 1893, be and the same is hereby repealed.

SEC. 232. That there be and is hereby created the office of Superintendent of Public Instruction, who shall be elected by the National Council at its regular session and who shall hold this office for a term of two years. He shall be installed in the same manner as other executive officers and until such installation he shall not be competent to perform the functions of his office. He shall have his office in the National Capitol building and shall be present at the sessions of the National Teachers' Institute. He shall be subject to laws regarding impeachment. He shall have authority to adopt rules and regulations not inconsistent with the laws of the Muskogee Nation for the government of schools established and maintained by the Nation; to authenticate his actions by the use of a seal; to make requisition on the executive department for funds necessary to the support of the schools; to prescribe and enforce a course of study in the several schools and furnish a series of text books one of which shall be the Bible; to prescribe and enforce rules for the examination of teachers and for the admission of pupils to the National boarding schools and such other high schools as may hereafter be established; to appoint teachers for the primary schools, and superintendents for the boarding and high schools, but the superintendents so appointed shall select and employ their own teachers; he shall examine applicants for the position of teachers and grant certificates according to qualifications; to revoke for immorality, incompetence or intemperance all certificates of whatsoever grade; to remove or discontinue any primary school which does not maintain a daily average of thirteen pupils during the winter months and fifteen during the summer months.

The Superintendent of Public Instruction shall appoint to each school three respectable citizens as a board of trustees who shall hold their office during their good behavior, but shall not be entitled to any compensation. The Superintendent of Public Instruction shall have complete control and supervision of all the schools and educational interests of the Nation at large, subject to such direction as may be imposed by law. The Superintendent of Public Instruction shall keep a correct record of all his transactions in a suitable book, which shall be open to any one for inspection; he shall report to the Principal Chief on or before the 15th day of September of each year a statement of the condition of the schools of the Muskogee Nation, accompanying his report with a tabular statement showing the number of schools in operation, number of children attending same, the amount of unexpended appropriation, if any, make estimates of funds required for support of schools the ensuing year, that the Council may have information upon which to base an appropriation; furnish blanks necessary to enable teachers and trustees to make their reports; to purchase the text books and distribute the same upon requisition of teachers. When a neighborhood shall make application to the Superintendent he shall grant permission for the establishment of a school provided there are not less than 15 pupils, and if a suitable school building with necessary fixtures be provided within six weeks after such permission is given he shall assign a teacher for the same. The Superintendent shall report at the close of each scholastic term to the Principal Chief the condition and progress of each school under his supervision, together with such suggestions and recommendations as he believes will improve the schools, which report or transcript thereof shall be furnished annually to the National Council of the Muskogee Nation within three days after the meeting of the regular session thereof. The Superintendent of public Instruction shall receive an annual salary of $800.00 and shall execute a bond of $2000.00 for a faithful performance of the duties of his office.

Approved November 5, 1896.

SALARIES—STANDING OFFICERS.

Sec. 233. From and after December 5, 1896, the salaries of the following named officers shall be and are hereby reduced to the amounts respectively set opposite their names:

1.	Principal Chief	from	$1200.00	to	$1000.00
2.	Second Chief	from	700.00	to	600.00
3.	Board of Education	from	600.00	to	500.00
4.	Prosecuting Attorney	from	200.00	to	100.00
5.	Supt. Boarding Schools, 100 p.,	from	750.00	to	600.00
6.	Supt. Boarding Schools, 50 p.,				500.00
7.	Creek Orphan Schools	from	700.00	to	600.00
8.	Colored Orphan School				500.00

Became a law by passing over Chief's veto November 7, 1896.

COMMITTEE ON WARRANTS.

PREAMBLE.

Whereas, The Muskogee Nation desires to ascertain the accurate amount of its national indebtedness, and prevent fraudulent manipulation of national warrants by changes on the face of said warrants from the original to greater amounts, and

Whereas, Our national warrants are made of a very inferior article of paper and subject to changes as to value by the use of chemicals without detection, and

WHEREAS, It is the desire of the Muskogee Nation to provide for the payment of its just indebedness, therefore,

SEC. 234. That the Principal Chief be and is hereby authorized and directed to appoint a committee composed of three compotent citizens, the appointment to be confirmed by the National Council, who shall be charged with the duty of calling in all outstanding warrants, and to examine them thoroughly as to their correctness by comparing them with the stubs from which they were issued, and with the appropriations made therefor, and after such investigation has been completed a full report thereof shall be made to the Principal Chief, who shall take up and destroy said warrants found to be correct, and shall issue in lieu thereof new warrants, in as large denominations as is practicable, to the holders of said old warrants.

The new warrants to be issued by the Chief, as herein provided, shall be made of the best quality of bank papers. printed or lithographed, designated by private and appropriate designs, and stamped with a cut stamp showing the numerals of each warrant. Said committee shall provide an erasable stamp which shall contain the word "void," with which all fraudulent warrants presented shall be stamped or branded. Said warrants shall be returned to the holders thereof.

SEC. 235. That the National Treasurer be and he is hereby directed to not pay only on the warrants that are herein provided for.

SEC. 236. That said committee shall receive a per diem of four ($4.00) dollars per day each for the time of their actual service.

SEC. 237. That the sum of one thousand ($1000.00) dollars be and is hereby appropriated in favor of the Principal Chief to be by him used for paying the per diem of said committee and such other expenses as shall be necessary to carry this act into effect.

SEC. 238. The new warrants herein provided for shall consist of two classes. One class shall be drawn on the school fund, and the other on the general fund, neither of which class shall be payable by the National Treasurer until endorsed by the National Auditor and by the holder thereof.

SEC. 239. All acts or parts of acts in conflict herewith are hereby repealed.

Approved November 10, 1896.

PASTURE, LARGE—TO BE TAKEN DOWN.

SEC. 240. That all pastures larger than one mile square now existing within the Muskogee Nation be and they are hereby declared to be in violation of our treaty stipulations, the principles of justice and equity, and are therefore subject to be taken down and removed from off the public domain of the Muskogee Nation, and

SEC. 241. That the Principal Chief be and he is hereby directed to notify all parties and companies, owners of pastures larger than one mile square, to take down and remove the same from off the public domain of the Muskogee Nation at once, and

SEC. 242. Any and all pastures larger than one mile square standing upon the public domain of the Muskogee Nation after the date of March 1, 1897, are hereby declared to be the common property of the Muskogee Nation, and the district attorneys of the several districts shall proceed forthwith to advertise and sell all such pastures as may be found in their respective districts, to the highest bidder for cash or national warrants in hand, conditioned that all such pastures shall be taken down and removed from off the public domain at once, and

SEC. 243. Any pastures having been sold as provided in the last preceding section of this act, found standing thirty days after such sale, then the Light Horsemen of the district wherein such pasture is found standing shall proceed forthwith to level the same to the ground, and

SEC. 244. That any prosecuting attorney confiscating and selling any pasture as provided in this act, he shall be allowed to keep as a personal fee 25 per cent. of all the moneys collected from such sales, the balance to be turned into the treasury of the Muskogee Nation.

SEC. 245. Nothing herein contained shall be construed as requiring the taking down or interfering with the large pastures built within ten miles of the border under contract with the Principal Chief in accordance with an act of the National Council entitled "Contract Pasture Law," approved November 3, 1892, and included in sections 341 to 354 inclusive, compiled laws, edition of 1893.

Approved November 10, 1896.

REPORT—COMMITTEE OF SIXTEEN.

OKMULGEE, I. T., Oct. 22, 1896.

To the National Council of the Muskogee Nation:

GENTLEMEN—Your special committee of sixteen have canvassed the subject laid before them by your honorable body, and fully recognizing the fact that the Nation is in the presence of a most important crisis, have the honor to present this their report and recommend its adoption.

Respectfully submitted, November 22, 1896.

D. M. HODGE,
Chairman Comittee of Sixteen.

G. W. GRAYSON, Clerk.

WM. MCCOMBS, Interpreter.

WHEREAS, The National Council of the Muskogee Nation, in regular session assembled at Okmulgee, did on the 12th day of October, 1896, pass the following resolution, to-wit:

Sec. 246. "*Be it Resolved by the National Council of the Muskogee Nation:* That a special joint committee be and is hereby appointed to be composed of seven members of the House of Kings and nine members of the House of Warriors whose duty it shall be to take into consideration the present relation our Nation sustains with the government of the United States, taking into consideration the reports of our national delegates to Washington, the commission of five (5) elected by the extraordinary session of the National Council of August 4, 1896, to confer with the Dawes Commission, and the report of our representatives in the late international council of the Five Civilized Tribes held at Eufaula, and report by recommending such legislation as they may deem necessary at as early a date as practicable to the present session of the National Council.

Approved October 12, 1896.

Roly McIntosh,
Acting Prin. Chief."

COMMISSION TO TREAT WITH DAWES COMMISSION.

PREAMBLE.

And Whereas, In pursuance of said resolution a special joint committee of sixteen on the state of the Nation was duly appointed, who have carefully considered the report of the delegation to Washington, that of the representatives to the international council held at Eufaula, 28th of July last, and that of the commissioners appointed by the extraordinary session of the National Council of August 4, 1896, as well as a communication from the Principal Chief submitting a letter from D. W. Bushyhead, chairman of the Cherokee commissioners appointed to confer with the Dawes Commission, together with such other matters as relate to the subject in hand. The probable effect and bearing of the subject matters of these several communications on the most vital interests of the Muskogee Nation has been considered as carefully by your committee as well as their ability and the lights before them permit; and

WHEREAS, The National Council of April 7, 1894, did, in answer to propositions made by the Dawes Commission, declare substantially that so radical a change in our land polity and political relations with the United States as that proposed by the said commission are incompatible with the best interests of the Muskogee Nation, they being a demand that we abandon our institutions and traditions, our system of land tenure in common, in exchange for which we are called upon to take upon ourselves a territorial or state form of government, subjecting us to a complex system of laws and conditions of which we have but little acquaintance or knowledge; and

WHEREAS, Under a later act of Congress the said Dawes Commissioners have made further overtures in the premises aforesaid, which if complied with, will entail untold inconveniences and hardships, together with great material loss caused by rearrangement of our homes, farms and improvements in conformity with government surveys; and

WHEREAS, It is not in accord with common reason to expect our people will enter into negotiations fraught with sacrifices of so great magnitude without satisfactory assurances that the government, as an earnest of its oft repeated declaration that the well being and prosperity of the Indian is the end desired to be attained in the proposed negotiations, was prepared to fully compensate them for the sacrifices they are called upon to make; and

WHEREAS, The change of government and institutions that we are asked to make are of most vital importance, imperatively demanding a due regard to the matter of time necessary for our people to acquaint themselves with and appreciate the new conditions proposed; and

WHEREAS, The negotiations proposed by the United States Commissioners do necessarily involve a settlement of all financial dues and claims against the United States government growing out of our treaties, which further emphasizes the need of time, therefore,

SEC. 247. *Be it Resolved by the National Council of the Muskogee Nation:* That there shall be a delegation or commission composed of five members and one interpreter, who shall be nominated by the Principal Chief and confirmed by the National Council, and who shall be selected with reference to the embracement of the confidence of the whole Muskogee people.

SEC. 248. *Be it further Resolved,* That the said commissioners or delegates herein provided for shall co-operate with the commissioners or delegates appointed by the other Indian Nations of the Indian Territory upon all matters respecting their common interests that may be proposed as subjects of negotiation by the United States Commission.

SEC. 249. *Be it furher Resolved,* That the Commissioners shall have power to confer with the Commissioners of the other Indian Nations and with the United States Commissioners known as the Dawes Commission relative to their mission to the five civilized tribes, and shall have power to propose and enter into such preliminary agreements with said United States Commissioners as they, upon conference and agreement with the other Indian representatives, shall deem wisest in the matters and things embraced in the foregoing preamble and resolutions.

SEC. 250. *Be it further Resolved,* That they may from time to time call in conference the Principal Chief on any subject the determination of which would in their judgment require his aid or advice. If from any cause he shall be unable to respond to such call, then the Second Chief shall represent him. But all their acts shall be subject always to the approval and ratification of the National Council.

SEC. 251. *Be it further Resolved*, That the delegates or commissioners shall for their services be paid a per diem of seven ($7.00) dollars during their terms of service as commissioners, but shall receive no mileage. They shall be provided with a fund of one ($100.00) dollars or so much thereof as may be necessary for incidental expenditures during their terms of service.

Approved October 28, 1896.

NUYARKA MISSION—COMMITTEE ON, CONTRACT CONCERNING.

SEC. 252. That the Principal Chief appoint and the National Council confirm two competent citizens, who, with the Superintendent of Public Instruction, shall go to Nuyarka Mission School, inspect the buildings and everything belonging to the school, take an inventory of the same and agree with the agent of the Presbyterian Home Mission Board upon a fair and reasonable basis, upon a compensation for the amount expended by the said Home Mission Board upon the buildings and furniture, and receive the said school and all its belongings from the agent of the said Presbyterian Home Mission Board and place it in the charge of the Superintendent of Public Instruction, and report their action to the next annual Council.

Approved March 27, 1897.

DUVAL, BEN T.—$500.00 OF HIS PAY MADE PREFERRED.

SEC. 253. That five ($500.00) hundred dollars of the amount appropriated November 2, 1896, in favor of Col. Ben T. DuVal for services to be rendered by him in resisting claimants to citizenship before the Dawes Commission and before the United States Court, be and the same is hereby declared preferred and the National Treasurer is hereby authorized to pay the full amount on five hundred dollars worth of these warrants out of any money not otherwise appropriated.

Approved March 27, 1897.

INTRUDERS—REQUEST TO HAVE THEM VACATE THE NATION.

SEC. 254. That the Principal Chief be and he is hereby directed to instruct the delegates elected to attend the present extraordinary session of Congress to wait upon the new Secretary of the Interior, and urge upon him to issue an order to all intruders in the Muskogee Nation to vacate the said Muskogee Nation at once.

Approved March 27, 1897.

GRAYSON, G. W.—RE-COMMISSIONED AS A DELEGATE TO WASHINGTON.

SEC. 255. G. W. Grayson, present delegate to Washington, D. C., shall be re-commissioned as such delegate to serve for the period of sixty (60) days from the first of April next, and the Principal Chief is hereby authorized to commission him to that office.

SEC. 256. The Principal Chief, Isparhecher, is hereby authorized to accompany the delegate provided in the foregoing act, with authority and power to do all things necessary to aid in effecting the objects with which the delegation is charged.

SEC. 257. If Congress shall appropriate the amount of Three Hundred Thousand Dollars, then the delegation and Principal Chief are hereby authorized to sign all papers and do whatever else is necessary to cause the early payment of said amount as intended by the act of appropriation, and their acts in that regard are to be regarded and accepted as the act of the Muskogee or Creek Nation.

SEC. 258. That there be and is hereby appropriated the sum of six hundred and twenty ($620.00) dollars each for

G. W. Grayson and Isparhecher, the same being for per diem for sixty days' service as delegation to Washington, D. C., and traveling expenses to and from said city, and five hundred dollars for contingent expenses incurred in the presentation of their work.

The above act became a law by being passed over the Chief's veto, March 27, 1897.

LICENSE LAW, AMENDMENT TO.

SEC. 259. That the license tax law found on page 86, Sec. 246, Ed. 1893, be so amended as to read: All legitimate business houses of whatsoever capacity or character engaged in the sale of all manner of dry goods, provisions, hardware, lumber, drugs, or any other article or articles known or designated as merchandise shall pay an annual tax of one per cent on the first cost of all goods or merchandise offered for sale, to be ascertained by personal inspection by the Tax Collector of the original invoices of purchase.

SEC. 260. All laws or parts of laws in conflict herewith are hereby repealed.

Approved March 24, 1897.

BALANCE OF $333,000.00, TO BE APPLIED ON CURRENT EXPENSES.

SEC. 261. That the Principal Chief be and he is hereby authorized and directed to draw a warrant on the United States Treasury for whatever balance may be left in the hands of the Secretary of the Interior after the payment of the three hundred and thirty-three thousand dollars on the debt of the Creek Nation as provided for in the Indian Appropriation Bill, and the said balance shall be applied to the payment of current expenses of the Creek government.

Approved March 27, 1898.

WARRANTS, CERTAIN—ISSUED BY THE CHIEF DECLARED VOID.

SEC. 262. *Be it Resolved by the National Council of the Muskogee Nation:* That the two warrants issued by the Principal Chief upon an appropriation made by the National Council of 1895 for the purpose of evicting intruders from the Nation, for thc per diem and incidental expenses of the two special commissioners to Washington, D. C., be and are hereby pronounced void and of no value and returned to the Executive Office to be destroyed.

Approved March 25, 1897.

NUYARKA MISSION—CONTRACT RELATIVE THERETO TO BE APPROVED BY THE NATIONAL COUNCIL.

SEC. 263. *Be it Resolved by the National Council of the Muskogee Nation:* That whatever agreement shall be made between the duly authorized persons on the part of the Muskogee Nation and the duly authorized representative of the Presbyterian Home Mission Board for the dissolution of the contract now subsisting between the said Nation and Board, including pecuniary settlements, shall first be submitted to the National Council and be approved by it befere the same shall be binding upon the Muskogee Nation.

Approved March 27, 1897.

COMMISSION TO TREAT WITH DAWES COMMISSION CONTINUED.

SEC. 264. That the delegation appointed by the last annual session of the National Council to treat with the Dawes Commission be and are hereby continued in authority under the provisions of all former laws prescribing their powers and duties.

SEC. 265. They are hereby further instructed to insist on indemnity to the Nation for the lands and moneys of which it has been deprived by the action of the United States in the enfranchisement of the Creek Freedmen in 1866.

SEC. 266. The delegation are hereby directed to submit to the National Council for its action any and all of their acts in any matter of negotiation that they may effect, and no act of negotiation shall be held to be valid for or against the Nation until after full and free consideration the same shall be approved and accepted by the National Council.

Became a law by limitation.

SESSION OF COUNCIL—FIXING TIME OF.

SEC. 267. That the law found on pages 5 and 6, Sec. 11, Pamphlet Laws, 1896, entitled an act limiting the periods of the sessions of the National Council, be and the same is hereby repealed, and the present session of Council shall be thirty days as heretofore with the privilege of adjourning sooner if the work is completed sooner.

Approved October 21, 1897.

PROSECUTING ATTORNEYS—TO TAKE A CENSUS OF INTRUDERS AND LIST OF STOCK BEING GRAZED UNLAWFULLY.

SEC. 268. The Prosecuting Attorneys of the several districts shall be required to ascertain the number of foreign cattle and horses now being grazed unlawfully in their respective districts, and the names of the owners of such cattle. They shall also ascertain the names of intruders residing unlawfully in their respective districts, giving the names of the heads of families, number of members of each family, and their post office address.

SEC. 269. The Principal Chief is hereby authorized and directed to appoint one prominent citizen of each district to assist the Prosecuting Attorney of his district, whose pay shall be two dollars per day.

SEC. 270. That there be and is hereby appropriated the sum of sixty dollars each in favor of said persons appointed to assist the Prosecuting Attorneys in these duties, making a total of three hundred and sixty dollars.

Sec. 271. The Prosecuting Attorneys and their assistants are required to report at as early a day as possible, and the Principal Chief is required to submit said reports to the Secretary of the Interior and ask immediate removal of said cattle, horses and intruders.

Approved October 21, 1897.

CHARGES AGAINST OFFICERS—TO BE SWORN TO.

Sec. 272. If any person or persons desire to prefer charges against any officer of this Nation, such person or persons shall be required to appear before a Supreme Judge or District Judge with witness or witnesses and shall take an oath that said charges are true and correct, and the Judge before whom the person or persons shall thus appear shall be required to keep as a matter of record for future reference and use all such charges and testimony which shall be submitted to the House of Warriors at the next regular session of Council.

Sec. 273. Upon the presentation of the charges duly signed by the witnesses and certified to by the Judge before whom they were sworn to, the Chief may suspend the accused officer, but he shall not suspend any officer upon charges which are not duly signed and sworn to. Any person or persons who may swear against the accused and shall swear differently at the trial of the accused shall be subject to the law governing perjury.

Approved October 27, 1897.

APPLICATION FOR PER CAPITA MONEY STOPPED.

Sec. 274. *Be it Resolved by the National Council of the Muskogee Nation:* That no application for any per capita payment shall be accepted or considered by the Council from and after the passage of this resolution.

Approved October 30, 1897.

MILEAGE OF SUPREME JUDGES.

SEC. 275. The members of the Supreme Court shall each receive mileage at the rate of ten cents per mile each way, coming and returning from the court; this act to commence so as to include attendance at the present term of the Supreme Court.

Approved October 28, 1897.

IMPEACH AN OFFICER—MAJORITY VOTE REQUIRED.

SEC. 276. All articles of impeachmement which shall arise in the House of Warriors and submitted to the House of Kings to decide whether the officer is guilty of the charge preferred against him, and after careful examination of the same the House of Kings decide to vote on the case, it shall take a majority vote of the House of Kings to impeach an officer.

Approved October 29, 1897.

AGREEMENT OF SEPTEMBER 27, 1897—REASONS WHY IT WAS REJECTED BY THE COUNCIL.

SEC. 277. *Be it Resolved by the National Council of the Muskogee Nation:* That in view of the fact that the agreement or treaty entered into between the United States and the Creek Nation by commissioners duly authorized thereunto on the 27th day of September, 1897, was, by joint resolution of the National Council, rejected as unsatisfactory to the Creek people, it is deemed proper that the reasons for such rejection should be publicly stated.

The most powerful consideration which induced the Creeks to remove from their country east of the Mississippi to their present home was the fact that the United States guaranteed them the unrestricted right of self-government and the peaceable occupancy of this country until they shall of their own accord make such changes in their relations to the Uniedt

States as they may deem for the betterment of their condition. It is necessary to recite a few well-known portions of the treaties now existing between the Creek Nation and the United States in order that the public may properly understand the guarantees upon which we have so far existed as a self-governing Nation.

Art. III, Treaty of 1834. "The United States will grant a patent in fee simple to the Creek Nation of Indians for the land assigned said Nation by this treaty or convention whenever the same shall have been ratified by the President and Senate of the United States; and the right thus guaranteed by the United States shall be continued to said tribe of Indians so long as they shall exist as a Nation and continue to occupy the country hereby assigned to them."

Art. IV, Treaty of 1856. "The United States do hereby solemnly agree and bind themselves, that no State or Territory shall ever pass laws for the government of the Creek or Seminole tribes of Indians; and that no portion of either of the tracts of country defined in the first and second articles of this agreement shall ever be embraced or included within, or annexed to, any Territory or State; nor shall either, or any part of either, ever be erected into a Territory without the full and free consent of the legislative authority of the tribe owning the same." Art. XV. of the same treaty guarantees to the Creeks "the unrestricted right of self-government and full jurisdiction over persons and property within their respective limits, excepting, however, white persons with their property, etc."

"The United States and the Creek Nation had a wise, definite and benevolent policy" in the grant of these lands west of the Mississippi. That policy was to secure to the Creeks a country in which they could grow up into a civilized, self-governing, prosperous and Christian people through laws to be enacted by their tribal legislators and adjudged and enforced by their tribal courts. That the result of this policy would ultimately break up tribal government and end in the absorption of the Indians by the great body of the citizens of the United States is not denied.

The only and final question to be decided now is, has the time actually arrived when that policy can be consummated at once without detriment to the best interests of the Creek people? All other questions are subordinate and merely incidental to this one great question.

It is proper to recite briefly the history of the Creek people. Prior to the late civil war between the States the Creeks were farmers and herdsmen, and a very respectable portion of them were slave-holders. They lived an easy and rather careless life. Education was not deemed of such high importance then as now. This was also true of the slave-holders of the Southern States. When the civil war broke out our country was between the contending forces. The people, in self-defense, abandoned their homes and their property and fled, some joining the Union army and others siding with the Confederacy. Thus was our country completely abandoned and all our property became a prey to speculators who followed the two great armies solely for gain. At the close of the war when the Creeks returned home they found the country a vast wilderness. The stock had all been driven away, the houses and fences burned by prairie fires, and their former places of residence almost beyond recognition. Then began the struggle for existence. In a country without money, everybody as poor as his neighbor, and no railroads or towns to bring trade or produce market, the people were indeed pioneers.

For nearly ten years after the war there were no railroads nor towns in this Nation. There were, however, established a few neighborhood and two boarding schools, which afforded only a few children the opportunities of acquiring a very elementary knowledge of books. This was the condition in this Nation when in 1889 that portion of Oklahoma which formerly constituted the west half of the Creek country was sold to the United States, and of the proceeds of said sale two millions of dollars was deposited with the United States Government as a permanent fund, and fifty thousand dollars annually of the interest thereon was set apart as a school fund; and immediately thereafter there were erected large brick and frame school buildings, and the neighborhood schools were increased to thrice their former number. Out of a total annual income or revenue of one hundred and sixty thousand dollars, eighty-four thousand dollars of it is expended annually for educational purposes. Every child of school age has now the chance of acquiring an education absolutely free to himself and parents. It is not believed that this system of education can be replaced by one better suited to the Creeks.

There are in this Indian Territory five separate local governments, neither one nor two of which can constitute a State sufficiently large to be admitted by Congress.

The movement toward a change of government in the Indian Territory should be simultaneous in all these Nations. Any treaty made with these Nations should be uniform in principle and equally protective of their various interests. The Indians will be the principal beneficiaries of any good that may result from a change of government, and they alone will suffer from the confusion and hardships which will necessarily follow the immediate breaking up of the tribal governments. The Congress of the United States has at no time been burdened with petitions from the great body of the white people in this country complaining of grievances or asking for the betterment of their condition; nor has any complaint gone up to Congress from the Indians of this Territory.

It is therefore incomprehensible to our people why this great pressure should be brought to bear upon them for the breaking up of their government.

The Commissioners on the part of the United States have threatened to disrupt our government if we do not by treaty at once agree to allot our lands and surrender our right of self-government.

The Congress of the United States has passed an act (Indian Appropriation Bill, approved June 7, 1897) which, after January 1st, 1898, deprives this Nation of the jurisdiction guaranteed to it by treaties. With this flaming sword as an everlasting threat hanging over the Nation, as it were, by a single thread, the Creek Commissioners were induced to sign the Agreement of September 27, 1897. This is a repetition of the coercion under which the Creek Delegation signed the treaty of Ft. Smith in 1866 in which it was agreed for the Creeks to sell the west half of the whole Nation, amounting to three million acres, at thirty cents an acre. There might have been some slight excuse at that time in using coercive measures, but now, thirty odd years since the great civil war ended, we have the right to demand justice and fair play.

It has been announced to be the purpose and desire of the United States to protect the interests of the majority of the Indians by devising a plan for the allotment of lands and by their admission as citizens of the United States. Upon a thorough understanding of the intent and scope of the treaty as interpreted and explained by the Commissioners it was rejected by a large majority of the members of the Council. No people can be accused of improper motives in an earnest desire to thoroughly consider their condition and endeavor to stand by those principles of government which have brought them prosperity and contentment. In the position thus taken the Creeks rely upon the honesty and fair-mindedness of the Commissioners of the United States and the members of Congress.

Approved November 3, 1897.

WARRANTS—MADE PREFERRED.

SEC. 278. All appropriations made by the present session of Council are made preferred, and the National Treasurer is hereby directed to pay the same in cash as soon as warrants are issued on same.

Became a law by limitation.

DELEGATION—TO WASHINGTON, D. C.

SEC. 279. That the creation of a delegation of three competent citizens, as provided by the act of December 2, 1897, to be nominated by the Principal Chief and confirmed by the National Council, be and is hereby authorized, whose duty, when so created, shall be to represent all interests of the Muskogee Nation at Washington, D. C., during the session of Congress which shall meet in December, 1897.

They shall use all proper efforts to cause a suspension, by order or special act, of the operation of the act of Congress of June 7, 1897.

The delegation elected under the provisions of this act are hereby required to act with energy and expedition in all their efforts to obtain all the objects desired by this act.

SEC. 280. That there be and is hereby appropriated the sum of four thousand, four hundred and fifty-two dollars for per diem for the delegates provided for in the foregoing section; six hundred dollars for traveling expenses, and five hundred dollars for contingent expenses of the same. The delegation, when elected, shall leave at once for their post of duty.

Approved December 7, 1897.

TELEPHONE COMPANY—ACT OF INCORPORATION.

SEC. 281. The following citizens, namely: Bluford Miller, N. B. Moore, Frederick B. Severs, and such other citizens of the Muskogee Nation as they may associate with themselves, are hereby granted a charter under the corporate name of "The Muskogee National Telephone Company," for the purpose of erecting, constructing, operating and maintaining a system of telephones within the Muskogee Nation, connecting the various towns of said Nation, and of erecting, constructing and maintaining a telephone system within the various towns of said Nation for hire; and, as such corporation, it shall have the power to make and use a common seal, to sue and be sued, to issue stock, and to make rules and regulations for the control and management of its affairs; and for the purpose of obtaining capital they shall have authority to admit as stockholders of said Company such non-citizens or legal association of non-citizens as they may elect; and said Company, chartered and organized by this act, shall have and is hereby granted the exclusive right and privilege to erect, construct, operate and maintain telephone lines within said Muskogee Nation for the period of its corporate existence.

SEC. 282. Articles of incorporation shall be filed with the Principal Chief in duplicate and shall set forth the names of the incorporators, the amount of the capital stock of said Company, and the number of shares into which the same is divided.

That when said articles of incorporation are approved by the Principal Chief, one copy shall be filed in the archives of the Muskogee Nation, and the other copy, together with a certificate of incorporation, shall be given to said Company, and the same shall be evidence of the corporate existence of said Company and of the right and privileges conferred by this act.

Sec. 283. Said Company shall have a sufficient right-of-way upon which to place its poles; and whenever practicable it shall run its lines along the roads and highways of said Nation.

Sec. 284. In consideration of the rights and privileges granted to said Company herein, said Company shall pay as annual tax, five per cent of its net profits to the Treasurer of the Muskogee Nation, and for the faithful payment of the same it shall file a bond in the sum of one thousand dollars with the Principal Chief of the Nation.

Sec. 285. The period of incorporation shall not exceed the term of from five to fifteen years, but that the same may be renewed. The incorporators shall act as officers and directors of said Company until their successors are elected and qualified.

Sec. 286. This act shall take effect from and after its passage and approval.

Approved December 7, 1897.

ATTORNEYS FOR THE NATION—ACT TO EMPLOY.

Sec. 287. That the National Delegates to Washington be, and they are hereby authorized and empowered, by and with the approval of the Principal Chief, to employ competent counsel, whose duty shall be, when so directed, to act as the legal representatives of the authorities of the Nation in the adjustment of all questions arising in the settlement of their National affairs before the departments of the government at Washington, the committees of Congress, or any of the courts of the United States.

Sec. 288. That twenty thousand dollars ($20,000.00) or so much thereof as shall be necessary, be and is hereby appropriated out of the general funds of the Nation, to be used as counsel fees and to defray other costs attending the proper prosecution of such business as shall be entrusted to their care. The said sum of twenty thousand ($20,000.00) dollars shall remain in the custody and care of the Principal Chief, and by him paid out, at such times as shall be necessary, to the attorneys employed under the provisions of this act; such payments being proportioned to the importance and amount of the work performed, or to be performed.

He shall render to the National Council a report of the particular service rendered by the attorney for the Nation, and the amount or amounts of money paid out therefor, together with a statement of all amounts or balances that may be remaining on hand.

Approved January 7, 1898.

WARRANT INVESTIGATION — TWO CITIZENS TO ASSIST U. S. OFFICERS.

SEC. 289. That the Principal Chief be and he is hereby instructed, authorized and empowered to appoint two competent and respectable citizens of the Muskogee Nation to accompany the special United States Agent in making a second investigation of Creek National warrants, and to aid said United States officer in searching for and designating all fraudulent warrants of the Creek Nation that may be in circulation.

SEC. 290. The persons appointed by the Principal Chief to accompany and aid the United States authorities in the investigation of Creek warrants shall receive a compensation of five ($5.00) dollars per day and traveling expenses incurred during actual service.

SEC. 291. That there be and is hereby appropriated the sum of one thousand ($1,000.00) dollars, or so much thereof as may be necessary, to be used by the Principal Chief in paying such persons as he may in accordance with this act.

SEC. 292. The Principal Chief shall keep a correct account of all moneys expended under and by virtue of this act, and report the same to the next regular session of Council, and the persons appointed by the Principal Chief shall also make a full report of their work to the next regular session of the National Council.

Approved January 7, 1898.

TRANSLATION OF CURTIS ACT—APPROPRIATION FOR.

SEC. 293. That out of the balance remaining in the treasury of the appropriation made for use in the work of evicting intruders, approved December 18, 1895, there be and is hereby diverted and appropriated two hundred and fifty-five and 70-100 ($255.70) dollars for payment of G. W. Grayson and D. C. Watson, who, under appointment of the Principal Chief, authorized by a resolution of a convention of representative men convened at the capital on the 20th day of July last, translated into Creek, prepared, mailed, and and in other ways distributed one thousand copies of translations of the Curtis Bill and the Creek-Dawes Agreement among the various towns of the Nation.

Approved October 12, 1898.

SESSIONS OF COUNCIL—FIXING LENGTH OF.

SEC. 294. That the law found on pages 5 and 6, Sec. 11, pamphlet edition of Creek Laws of 1896, entitled an act limiting the period of sessions of the Creek National Council, be and is hereby repealed, and the present and all subsequent sessions of the Creek Council shall be thirty days, with the right to adjourn sooner if it be the pleasure of both Houses and the Principal Chief.

Approved October 14, 1898.

POLICE FORCE—AT OKMULGEE.

SEC. 295. During the present and all subsequent sessions of the National Council the said Council shall, for the maintenance of good order within the limits of the capital town of Okmulgee, have the power and is hereby charged with the duty of providing means and methods necessary to preserve order and decorum therein. It may call upon the Judge of the District to furnish his entire Light Horse Company to remain in attendance during the sessions of the Council, performing such police services and exercising such power as shall be necessary to keep order, and they shall be paid two dollars per diem in addition to their regular annual salary.

If for any cause it shall be impracticable for said officers to serve in said capacity, then the Council shall call upon the Judge of the District to appoint such number of other men as it may designate, who shall be paid two dollars per day. Any nuisance in the form of gambling; all halls or stands vending cider or other drinks that seem to intoxicate, or which become a place where drunken or boisterous men habitually congregate and become noisy and boisterous by either loud and unnecessary whooping, swearing, yelling or shooting of guns, shall be and are hereby made subjects to be abated by the police force operating under this act.

Said officers are hereby invested with power to execute the law of the Nation upon all persons found selling any intoxicating drinks, the same as is required of the Light Horsemen in such cases.

SEC. 296. If any person violates the provisions of this law he shall be taken before the Judge of the District and fined in the sum of five dollars, and no property shall be exempt under this law. If the person is unable to pay the fine at once then the Judge shall give him not more than three days in which to pay the fine, and he shall be released under bond executed before the Judge, and all fines collected by the police officers shall be turned over to the Committee on Capitol Building for use on said building.

SEC. 297. If any of the police officers shall become intoxicated they shall not be paid for their services as police and shall be removed from office.

SEC. 298. The jurisdiction and authority of the police officers authorized under this act shall extend over the ground in Okmulgee covered by the distance of one-half mile from the Capitol building north, south, east and west.

Approved October 10, 1898.

OATH OF OFFICE—BY WHOM TO BE ADMINISTERED.

SEC. 299. The President of the House of Kings shall hereafter have authority to administer the oath of office to members of the National Council and to all executive or other officers who may be elected or appointed in this Nation and who are required to take the oath of office before entering upon the duties of their office.

Approved March 21, 1899.

ISPARHECHER.

Approved April 18, 1899.

WILLIAM McKINLEY.

MILEAGE—DOUBLE.

SEC. 300. It is the sense of the Council that as the regular session of 1899 was divided into two parts thus necessitating going to and from the Capital twice of the members, clerks and interpreters, that the mileage of members should be paid for both trips.

Approved December 2, 1899.

ISPARHECHER.

DELEGATION—TO WASHINGTON, D. C.

SEC. 301. *Be it Resolved by the National Council of the Muskogee Nation:* That there be appointed a delegation to be composed of five competent citizens of the Nation who shall have full power to agree with Congress on the modification of the last agreement submitted to it which will secure to us the right guaranteed to us by the agreement of September 27, 1897, and outlined in the platform of July 4, 1899.

SEC. 302. *Be it further Resolved:* That the delegation herein provided for shall act under such further instructions as the National Council may adopt for their guidance, and any agreement or modification of existing agreements that may be agreed upon by Congress and our delegation shall be submitted to the National Council for ratification, and shall not be binding upon the Creek Nation until ratified by the National Council.

SEC. 303 *Be it further Resolved:* That the delegation to Washington are hereby authorized to call the Principal Chief to Washington whenever they may deem his presence and assistance necessary to their work.

Approved December 16, 1899.

APPROPRIATION—FOR DELEGATION, 1900.

SEC. 304. That there be and is hereby appropriated the sum of six thousand and five hundred ($6,500.00) dollars, or so much thereof as may be necessary, for per diem, traveling and other expenses of G. A. Alexander, D. M. Hodge, Isparhecher, A. P. McKellop and Cub McIntosh, delegates appointed by the Principal Chief, P. Porter, and confirmed by the National Council, to represent the Muskogee Nation at Washington, D. C., during the present session of Congress, in the matter of the modification, rearrangement and ratification by Congress of the agreement between the United States and the Muskogee Nation entered into February 1, 1899, and for the purpose of representing the Muskogee people in all other matters effecting their interests.

Sec. 305. That there be and is hereby appropriated the sum of one thousand ($1,000.00) dollars, or so much thereof as may be necessary in favor of P. Porter, Principal Chief of the Muskogee Nation, for traveling and other necessary expenses in case it shall become necessary for him to go to Washington, D. C., to assist the delegation in their work as provided by resolution of the Council of December 14, 1899.

The expenditure of the above amounts shall be accounted for to the Principal Chief by vouchers, and shall be paid in accordance with such rules and regulations as may be prescribed by the Secretary of the Interior for the disbursement of Creek funds.

Approved December 16, 1899.

P. PORTER.

Approved subject to the limitations that the expenditures for the purpose indicated shall not exceed the sum of four thousand, eight hundred and twenty-five ($4,825.00) dollars.

March 20, 1900. WILLIAM McKINLEY.

INDEX.